Kabbalah and the Power of Dreaming

"Many cultures believe that during a dream the soul leaves the dreamer's body and journeys to other worlds, possibly visiting the imaginal realm where the dreamer seems to break free of the limitations of time and space. In *Kabbalah and the Power of Dreaming* Catherine Shainberg not only takes us into that realm, she provides insights and a travel guide. Not since the time of Joseph and his prophetic dreams has such a well-written story-telling guidebook been offered."

Fred Alan Wolf, Ph.D., author of *Mind Into Matter*

"A brilliantly articulated exploration of the elusive mystery of dreams and imagination, and how they dance both sides of the veil between fantasy and reality. Combining ancient mystical wisdom with contemporary metaphor, Catherine Shainberg not only illuminates our understanding about the phenomenon of dreaming and its impact on the waking world, but also offers us ample user-friendly exercises and meditations to experience the wisdom of both. Shainberg is a foremost disciple of one of the few and most notable women kabbalists, Colette Aboulker-Muscat, herself a descendant and student of the thirteenth-century Rabbi Yitzchak Saggei Na'hor (known as Isaac the Blind) and of his mystery school. Like her teacher Colette, Shainberg has helped innumerable people through her healing work with imagery and dream. In *Kabbalah and the Power of Dreaming* she has, for the first time, shared with all of us the heretofore inaccessible wisdom of dream from the rich kabbalistic tradition of her teacher and her people. This is a book that delivers everything its title promises; it is an important addition to the classical literature of Jewish spiritual wisdom."

Rabbi Gershon Winkler, author of
Kabbalah 365: Daily Fruit from the Tree of Life

"Catherine Shainberg contributes a fresh, creative, and innovative approach to dreaming and imagination through the practice of waking dream. In doing so she brings alive the ancient wisdom of prophetic Kabbalah in a practical and readily usable way. *Kabbalah and the Power of Dreaming* deserves to be read and enjoyed; its reader will be richly rewarded with the spiritual view of life it provides."

Gerald Epstein, M.D., author of *Healing Visualizations:
Creating Health Through Imagery*

"The medieval system of Jewish Kabbalah taught that a more real world than our own lies behind the common one of day-to-day experience. Through lifelong routines of meditation and visualization, kabbalists drew on the insights of that other world. Now Catherine Shainberg, psychologist, poet, and dream specialist, provides a warm, richly detailed guide to this kind of thinking for the seekers of today. Her book opens with a moving account of her own search for bearings, then spans the ocean of kabbalistic tales and models. It is a heartfelt and generous guide to the questing imagination and, inevitably, to deepened relationships with others on the same trail."

Eleanor Munro, author of *Originals: American Women Artists*

"*Kabbalah and the Power of Dreaming* is a magnificent guide to putting soul back in the body and walking a path with heart. Catherine Shainberg is a profound spiritual teacher who reminds us that dreaming is not only about what we do when we sleep but about waking up to a deeper life by remembering and navigating from our sacred purpose. It instructs us on how to tap into our Source energy—including the images that speak to the body that can make it well—and informs us on how we can be present at the place of creation. Her book contains a panoply of practical exercises for transforming fear and anger into heart-centered energy, thereby liberating ourselves from the rule of habit and healing the wound between Earth and Sky. I highly recommend this book."

Robert Moss, author of *Dreamways of the Iroquois:
Honoring the Secret Wishes of the Soul*

"Catherine Shainberg's book begins with an entrancing account of her personal entry into the world of dreams and images, and reveals how she discovered her own great teacher of images and dreams, the renowned kabbalist Colette Aboulker-Muscat. Shainberg draws upon many years of experience to guide us through the possibilities of inner growth through dreamwork, offering exercises along the way that are intriguing and seem likely to open the mind and heart further and further. The power of dreaming is something I've come to appreciate more and more in my own life, and Shainberg's book does justice to that power. She is on a path of great beauty."

Rodger Kamenetz, author of *The Jew in the Lotus*

Kabbalah
and the
Power of
Dreaming

Awakening the
Visionary Life

CATHERINE SHAINBERG, PH.D.

Inner Traditions
Rochester, Vermont

Inner Traditions
One Park Street
Rochester, Vermont 05767
www.InnerTraditions.com

Note to the reader: This book is intended to be informational and should not be considered a substitute for advice or therapeutic counseling from a professional psychologist, who should be consulted by the reader in all matters related to his or her psychological health and particularly with regard to any symptoms that may require diagnosis and attention.

Library of Congress Cataloging-in-Publication Data
Shainberg, Catherine.
  Kabbalah and the power of dreaming : awakening the visionary life / Catherine Shainberg.
      p. cm.
  Summary: "An exposition of the powerful, ancient Sephardic tradition of dreaming passed down from the renowned 13th-century kabbalist Isaac the Blind"— Provided by publisher.
  ISBN 1-59477-047-6 (pbk.)
  1. Dreams. 2. Dreams—Religious aspects—Judaism. 3. Cabala—History.
4. Meditation—Judaism. 5. Kavvanot (Cabala) 6. Jewish meditations. I. Title.
  BF1078.S445 2005
  154.6'3—dc22
                                                        2004024492

Printed and bound in the United States at Lake Book Manufacturing, Inc.

10 9 8 7 6 5 4 3 2 1

Text design and layout by Priscilla Baker
This book was typeset in Sabon, with Delphin and Avenir as display typefaces

"Not Waving but Drowning" by Stevie Smith, from *The Collected Poems of Stevie Smith* © 1972 by Stevie Smith. Reprinted by permission of New Directions Publishing Corp.

All lines from "Mirror" from *Crossing the Water* by Sylvia Plath. © 1963 by Ted Hughes. Originally appeared in *The New Yorker*, reprinted by permission of HarperCollins Publishers, Inc.

"Oceans" reprinted from *The Winged Energy of Delight: Selected Translations*, Robert Bly, HarperCollins Publishers, New York, 2004. Copyright 2004 Robert Bly. Used with his permission.

In Memoriam

The author with Colette, in her garden in Jerusalem, 1979

To my teacher Colette Simhah Aboulker-Muscat I dedicate this book, a book that she never got to read. Colette passed away in the afternoon of November 25, 2003, at her home in Jerusalem. She was 94. The night before she died, she was still receiving visitors and dispensing wisdom and exercises. I had just arrived from the States. We spent the morning together reconnecting. Then she sent me away and she died.

"The Tzaddikim (sages) who have died are present in this world to a greater extent than when they were alive."

ZOHAR III, 70B.

Colette's teachings live on in what you are about to read.

About the School of Images

The School of Images (SOI) is a Kabbalah school founded to advance awareness of imagination as the foremost language for instantaneous insight and transformation. The school, founded by Catherine Shainberg in 1982, teaches the techniques of dreaming, visualization, and revelation to gain access to the forgotten source of the imagination within, to cleanse, revivify, and motivate the individual.

The School of Images derives its methods from early Jewish, Sephardic, and Mediterranean sources. The lineage dates back to two kabbalists, Isaac the Blind of Provence and Rabbi Jacob Ben Sheshet of Gerona, Spain, who lived and practiced Kabbalah in the thirteenth century. The last lineage holder, Madame Colette Aboulker-Muscat, adapted these ancient methods to meet the needs of a contemporary, global society.

In line with her teacher, Catherine Shainberg's work is experiential. Some of the exercises are based on text but, in contrast to other Kabbalistic ways, in this method there is no direct study or analysis of text and no permutation of letters (the technique known as *gematria*). The work is pure Kabbalah (*kabbalah* means "receiving"), in that one "receives" from their inner gazing. Thus, SOI's brand of Kabbalah is not a difficult system to access, but rather an exploration of the imaginal field whose language is common to people of all denominations. Each imagery exercise is a peerless tool for instantaneous vision, transformation, and healing.

The mission of the school is to teach the use of the imagination for creative, healing, and transformational purposes. Its goal is for people of all languages and creeds to practice imagery. Its belief is that this global language has the power to unite all peoples while allowing each of us to follow our own unique path.

To receive more information about SOI or to contact us:
Go to www.schoolofimages.com

Contents

List of Exercise Reference Guides

Acknowledgments

Sam Green

Didi Conn

Denise DeBaun

Jane Lahr

My son Sam

all my students

Celia Candlin

Frank Trujillo

Tom Roberts

Tom Schmall

Gay Walley

Thank you

Jeanie Levitan

Arthur Kurzweil

Jon Graham

Anne Dillen

Ehud Sperling

Nadia Cret

Jewish Theological Society

Malina Isham

Tabita Shalem

Prologue

"I sleep but my heart is awake."

SONG OF SONGS 5:2

All my life I have been a dreamer. As a child when I heard music, I'd see images in Technicolor. I lived with fairies and angels. I entered into other people's dreams. I "saw" these people and helped them in my dreaming. My mother said I was dreaming my life away. She wanted me to be practical. I thought I *was* practical.

For instance, I knew that dreaming would not be an acceptable substitute for regular schoolwork. So I had this system where I listened with one ear and imagined that what the teacher said went into a pocket in my mind, like a camel's second stomach. I had learned that if I visualized this pocket, I could always recall the information later on when it came time to answer questions.

Meanwhile, my *real* life went on in another world. Sitting in class I would let my gaze go up to a corner of the ceiling and proceed to dream all day long and no one was the wiser. As a young girl, when I thought about going to college, I couldn't imagine what I could study that would be as interesting to me as the beautiful images and sounds I found in my dreams. Then, as I grew up, the beautiful images and music of the inner worlds that belong to artists became real to me. I decided to study art.

* * *

Paris is filled with churches, palaces, gardens, statues, fountains. At every street corner there is something to feast one's eyes on. As an art student I would wander into the Louvre to look at paintings. Often, after studying a painting, I would have to go home to calm down. Everything felt so intense.

I wondered why some colors and shapes moved me so much while others had no effect on me. In the abundance of visual delights and possibilities that were all around me, I began playing with shapes and colors.

For instance, I'd blot out a lemon in a painting by Matisse and everything would go dead in the picture. When I viewed a photograph of *The Blind Leading the Blind* by Bruegel, printed reversed, the blind men in the painting, instead of tumbling inexorably to the picture's right as in the original, turned instead to the left where they awkwardly looked at a hole in the ground: a completely different effect.

I wanted to know if there were laws describing how shapes, colors, and spatial directions affect our emotions. I knew that certain colors in my dreams frightened me, while others made me very happy.

I knew that whenever I entered Notre Dame de Paris, the gothic cathedral that soars above the Seine, my body would feel lighter and grow tall, serene. If I stood with my back to a painting by Cézanne, not knowing it was in the room, the skin on my back would start to tingle. I was able to identify the painter without even turning to look.

Were other people this sensitive? Were they possibly as sensitive but didn't know it? I was aware that people often said that some places made them feel good while other places oppressed them. Where could I find out more about this kind of experience? And what would I do with the knowledge once I gained it?

I wanted to write my doctoral dissertation about these issues but my teachers were unimpressed and they steered me towards more tangible subjects. I quit.

Imagine a dreamer alone in Paris, no job, no purpose. What does she do? Well, dream of course! I dreamt and the dreams told me what to do. However, I did not receive this guidance without the price of some psychological pain, as I hadn't yet learned to fully trust my dreams. The result was that I couldn't do what I was guided to do without feeling a lot of trepidation and fear about my future.

Facing each day in a state of uncertainty about basic life decisions is difficult even when we are *accomplished* dreamers. I took a job in publishing and met a young man, a Jew from North Africa.

Listening to his ideas, meeting his friends, all Mediterranean Jews, and talking with them, I was overwhelmed by the fluidity of their thinking, the strength of their imagination, and their kindness. I wanted to immerse myself in their world. I went to Egypt. I went back four times, and then I visited Lebanon, Syria, and Jordan. I couldn't get enough of these countries. They felt like home.

I come from an old aristocratic French family from the Dordogne. At the time, one of my explanations for my newly discovered passion for the Middle East was that some gene from an ancestor who had gone to the Crusades had been stirred.

Then outside circumstances, together with more dreaming, led me to my next move, Israel. I went to a kibbutz in the desert. Now I *really* didn't know what I was doing! Instead of attending the Ivy League college in the States where I had been offered a scholarship, I was picking fruit in the Negev.

I had no profession, no money, no prospects, and I didn't speak Hebrew. I stayed two years. They were the worst years of my life. The dreams stopped. I was in the dark, desperate and friendless. Going home wasn't an option. I became a recluse.

There was a group of young French Jews on the kibbutz. One Sabbath, friends of theirs came to visit from Jerusalem. Although I was in my usual funk that day, hearing them speak French acted on me like a magnet and I found myself mingling with them on the lawn.

I asked a man named Eli about the French community in Jerusalem. He told me it revolved around a woman by the name of Colette. As I heard the name, C_O_L_E_T_T_E, my mind exploded into white light. I saw a huge brilliant star and knew, without a doubt, that I had to meet this lady.

I knew nothing about her and Eli could tell me nothing more than that he had once met her. But on hearing her name, my dreaming had started again! I took Eli's phone number and the next chance I had I went to Jerusalem.

Well, nothing is easy, and we are tested all along the way. Eli didn't show up for our appointment. I journeyed six times to Jerusalem, the Yom Kippur War came and went, and still he would not take me to meet her. It took me a long time to figure out he was afraid that when he did take me to Colette, she might ignore us both.

Meanwhile, my desire to meet her increased. With only pennies in my pocket, I left the kibbutz and moved to Jerusalem. Now Eli had no choice. He had to face the fact that I was the crazy girl who insisted on being introduced to this charismatic woman, no matter how he felt about it. He finally took me to meet Colette.

The street was very quiet. Wisteria and bougainvillea blossomed everywhere. The entrance to her house was half-hidden by wild roses and jasmine. The gate was blue. There were stone steps leading down into her garden. The door was ajar.

We passed into semi-darkness where a tall mirror greeted us with our own reflections. We moved on into a small salon filled with cushions and oriental rugs, with a beautiful Arabic copper chandelier hanging overhead.

A voice called us into the room that served as Colette's bedroom but looked more like the reception room of a queen. Colette lay on her bed, propped up by more pillows. The room was decorated with rich, sixteenth-century Algerian wood paneling worthy of a museum. She waved us to chairs set by her bed. "What do you want?" she said to me.

Without missing a beat, my dreaming voice spoke up, "Teach me how images move people!"

Colette laughed. "I have waited for you a long time!"

Who was Colette? I didn't even bother to ask; she was so completely familiar to me. At our first appointment she didn't seem very interested in my story either, but rather in the images I saw in my mind's eye: "Close your eyes, breathe out slowly three times, imagine . . . and then tell me what it is you see."

I realized later that my images told her all she needed to know about me and where I was headed. My images were like a map to her, a book she could read from to guide me. With her feedback I felt supported; comfortable in allowing myself to be led by what I "saw." A great adventure had begun! This exploration of myself would bring me further than I had ever thought possible, even to the exploration of universal structures and concepts.

Colette forbade me to ask questions or to read anything having to do with imagery, dreams, or myth. The images elicited by my reading would get mixed up with my inside images, she told me, and I would never know my true self. *I was the book, and the text was in me.*

Who was Colette? My eyes told me that she was a grande dame. This I recognized by her queenly posture and imperious manner, and also by her grace and attention to others that reminded me of my great-aunts and great-uncles. After the 1967 Six-Day War, Colette didn't once leave her house or her street, in order to be available to all those who might need her.

For me she was a powerful magnet, both motherly and terrifying. In her presence I felt totally naked and exposed. I was fascinated and head over heels in love. Colette gave me her dead daughter's clothing and took me into her heart and her life. I soon learned that Colette came from an ancient and famous Jewish family of doctors from Algiers. Her father, a neurosurgeon known throughout all of North Africa, had been nicknamed "le grand Marabou" (the great holy man), by the Arabs. Colette had been her father's personal assistant for fourteen years, during which time he trained her to observe his patients and then diagnose them. In all the years I spent with Colette, I never knew her to err when making a diagnosis.

Before deciding to consecrate her life to helping people, Colette had become an accomplished dancer, musician, and sculptress. Later, she studied in Paris with Dr. Desoille who had developed *le reve éveillé dirigé* ("Directed Waking Dream Therapy"). After obtaining her psychology degree, Colette worked in the psychiatric ward of the Algiers Hospital.

Because Colette felt that the Desoille techniques were limited, she went on to develop her own methods, which were informed by her family's ancestral imagery practices as well as by her own creative genius. Thus, she crafted the coherent and powerful overarching system that I will be describing to you in this book.

Colette holds lineage descent, on both her mother and father's side, from an ancient line of Sephardic kabbalists. Rabbis Isaac the Blind of Provence, the first recorded medieval kabbalist, and Jacob ben Sheshet, one of the leading lights of the Gerona circle of kabbalists and a follower of Isaac the Blind, are her direct ancestors. They are best-known for their fearless exploration of the mysteries which they plummeted through mystical exercises whose origins probably date back to the Merkavah Kabbalah.

This most ancient form of Kabbalah, traces of which can be found in Midrashic and Talmudic texts as well as in the Heikhalot and Merkavah literature, and in numerous Apocrypha manuscripts such as the Hebrew Book of Enoch, was practiced during the first and second centuries by commoners and Talmudic sages alike, among them Rabbi

Akiba, the foremost scholar of his time. The practitioner's task was to visualize ascending through the heavenly spheres, often seen as different palaces (the Heikhalot), to the chariot-throne (Merkavah) upon which the practitioner, if he reached that stage, "saw" the Image of the Lord (sometimes called the Kavod) in "the likeness as the appearance of a man above it" (Ezekiel 1:26).

In their literature, the kabbalists describe an unbroken chain of transmission (for instance, the Zohar, the most influential of all kabbalistic texts, was attributed by its author Moses de Leon to the second-century sage, Simeon Bar Yochai) dating back to Talmudic and Biblical times. Certainly the Hebrew Bible abounds in revelations, from the visions of prophets such as Ezekiel, Elija, and Enoch to the dreams of the patriarchs Abraham, Jacob, and Joseph, and the visionary experiences of a Moses, Samuel, or Jonah. It is clear, from perusing the Bible text, that the most prevalent form of communication with the Divine, in Biblical times, was the visionary process.

Thus, in line with her ancestors' practices, Colette's work is experiential. Some of her exercises are based on text but, in contrast to other kabbalistic methods, in her method there is no direct study or analysis of text, no permutation of letters (the technique known as "Gematria"), no study of the "Tree of Life" with its ten spheres of energy.

Colette's work is pure Kabbalah; (Kabbalah means "receiving"), in that one "receives" from one's inner gazing. Therefore, her brand of Kabbalah is not an arcane, difficult to access system, but an exploration of the imaginal field whose language is common to people of all denominations.

I wasn't a Jew when I met Colette, and she never spoke to me of Judaism. It was only when my images told me to look at Judaism that she opened some books and showed me kabbalistic texts. What I read there confirmed all that I had been discovering in myself through my imagery practice. At that point I converted to Judaism because, clearly, I was a Jew. Other students discovered that they were Buddhists or Sufis or Christians. Our souls spoke to us through our images and we were led to our true destinies.

Jewish Kabbalah is traditionally transmitted only to the men. However, as is sometimes the case in Sephardic families, the women in Colette's family were also encouraged to learn and to play active roles. Colette's illustrious family also included Dona Gracia Mendoza, the greatest Jewish woman figure of the Renaissance, in its lineage. More recently, Colette's grandmother was a famous teacher who held court, in her gardens, with the rabbis and important men of Algiers.

While still very young, Colette received, through a laying on of hands by her grandfather, the family's blessing to carry on the teachings of their lineage. She had three distinct beauty marks (one on her third eye, one on her left palm, and one on her heart) which, according to family tradition, were physical signs preordaining that she was born to save the Jews and the world.

And indeed, together with her teenage brother Jose Aboulker, Colette would go on to organize the resistance movement in North Africa, which led to the landing of American troops near Algiers, subsequently contributing to the end of World War II. Colette was the "Voice of Freedom" on Algerian Radio during the war. She was a decorated war hero; you can read her story in the history books of that epoch.

Colette later became the president of WIZO (Women's International Zionist Organization) in North Africa. She was sought out by Jews, Muslims, and Christians alike, and was named the official exorcist of the Catholic Church. The Rosicrucians awarded her their Medal of Honor, which only four women, among them Eleanor Roosevelt, had received before her.

With her husband Arie Muscat, a *shaliach* (a roaming ambassador for the State of Israel) and later, state controller for the city of Jerusalem, Colette worked diligently for the cause of Israel. Every Saturday night at their home in Jerusalem, she and Arie held an open house to celebrate the ending of the Sabbath.

People traveled from all over the world to sit in Colette's presence and receive her teachings. Toward the end of her life, she made her work with terminally ill patients a priority. Many of them, having done her exercises, are still among us today. On the three-thousand-year jubilee celebrating King David's reign, the city of Jerusalem honored her unique contributions and accomplishments by awarding her the prestigious Medal of the Beloved.

These are only the bare bones of Colette's life. It would take me a book to tell you all that she accomplished in her lifetime. She changed *my* life, for one thing, as she did the lives of countless other people. As she had been known to say, *we*, her students, were her true medals.

Before long, Colette was sending me out as her ambassador, to bring her exercises and comforting words to sick people, wounded soldiers, and mentally ill patients in the hospitals of Jerusalem. On a little scrap of paper, she would write out an exercise, an idea, or a direction which I was to work from. Soon, with her blessing, I began teaching a form of bodywork based on the study of movement in the Hebrew Bible stories. To respond to my students' needs, I developed imagery for all forms of physiological difficulties and disorders.

Whether I was sitting in Colette's garden or branching out to serve the community, I blossomed and thrived. I had found, both within myself and outside of myself, *my* Garden of Eden.

Colette once said to me: "Walk before me, you must become greater than I!"

Who can match such generosity?

To Colette the beloved I dedicate this book. She is my mother and I am her daughter. We are forever linked by Spirit. She taught me to trust what I already knew, and she taught me far more, some of which you will read in the pages of this book.

Colette loved to tell stories about her ancestors. These stories are parables and sources of inspiration to her students around the world who are "as numerous as the grains of sand and the stars in the sky." I believe of a great teacher that, for every student they teach in person, there are a thousand more who they counsel in the dream time.

The most amazing part of the story to me is that Colette was *my* dream come true!

Later details came out that only reinforced our connection. Colette's family home in Oran, Algeria, where she grew up during part of her childhood, was across the street from my mother's home! Colette had gone to the same school as my mother and my aunts, she knew them all.

And how does one explain the fact that I look so much like someone from Colette's family? A dream-transferred gene must have hopped from Colette's house into my mother. Journeys spiral back to their origins, with something added at each turn on the way. Dreaming is often more mysterious than we may even dream it to be!

Wake Up and Dream

"Whenever you wish that Elijah becomes visible to you, concentrate on him. . . . There are three ways of seeing him: in a dream; while awake and greeting him; while awake, greeting him, and being greeted in return."

JOSEPH CARO

There are many books about dreams. Why another? Because this book is not about dreams, it is about the *act* of dreaming. We may not be aware of it at every moment, but at every moment we are dreaming. You are dreaming as you read these lines, or when you stand waiting for the bus, or speak to a friend in a cafe, or when you work or cook, talk, or just do nothing.

Dreaming emanates from our right brain which, along with the rest of our brain, never stops emitting nerve impulses. This is a natural result of being alive. Like breathing, it goes on day and night.

Our night dreams are only one particular form of dreaming, one which we recognize easily because dreams which arise when we are asleep are a socially acceptable part of our subconscious. If we pay attention to our dreams, they will help to make us aware of the dreaming that goes on at *all* times.

I once received a visit from a man who was writing a book about quantum physics and dreams. He wished to ask a question. He had recently interviewed a druid, a modern day Celtic priest, for whom he had great respect. The druid had emphatically declared that there was no difference between night dreams and our daytime condition, we dream at *all* times. He was curious to know what I, a dream specialist and a psychologist to boot, thought about that.

At the time, I was surprised that the druid was the only person this man could find who would tell him that dreaming is an uninterrupted brain activity. Not for the first time I found myself wondering if the act of dreaming was not being treated by the world of science as a well-kept secret, bits and pieces of which exist but are never offered up as a complete system.

TWO DIFFERENT LANGUAGES

I always tell my students there are two great paths to follow in learning: the path of liberation through the *verbal* mind, and the path of liberation through the *imaginal* mind. This can be exemplified by two Buddhist ways: Zen Buddhism and Tibetan Buddhism.

Zen teaches its disciples to sit and watch, with detachment, the movements of the mind. At intervals, short paradoxical riddles called "koans" are given as subjects for meditation to test the follower's progress. Thus, teaching is done through appealing to the verbal mind and then, through the paradoxical intensity of the koan, dissolving habitual patterns of thought.

In contrast, Tibetan Buddhism enlists the *imaginal* mind of its followers. It accepts the forest of images that we live in and teaches its adepts to plunge in, travel through, and eventually come out on the other side of the forest. The ultimate goal of both great paths is enlightenment by detachment from all forms, *verbal* or *imaginal*.

Our way, as you may have already guessed, emphasizes the imaginal mind. Fearlessness and detachment are attained using both approaches, and everyone in real life has to make use of both paths. Nevertheless, on the level of simple physiological functioning, different individuals almost always have a predilection for one approach or the other. We are either drawn to the left brain (verbal) or to the right brain (imaginal).

Each side of the brain is associated with specific tendencies in behavior. The left brain is abstract and talks of mind, the right brain is spatial and speaks of body. It is important, therefore, that the language we use be congruent with the type of thinking that we are addressing.

There is a lot of confusion about this. The mind-body problem has produced much verbal garbage and little clarity. Inherent in the dichotomy is the existence of two distinct worlds which interrelate but do not use the same language. It's abundantly clear what we mean by "language" when speaking of the left brain. But what do we mean when speaking of the "language" of the right brain?

THE RIGHT BRAIN LANGUAGE

The right brain doesn't "think," it experiences. Its realm is the body, its language is formed with images. By images, I mean the process by which the right brain translates our sensory experiences into awareness.

For example, if someone attacks you, you might see red. This is not a metaphor, you actually do "see red." And often the "seeing" is more elaborate than this; you might see the attacker as a fiery monster. However, the image is so fleeting that it often slips from our consciousness, just like a night dream tends to do, before we have had time to "know" it.

Can we *speak* about images? Can we take an experience that is complete in itself and turn it into the sequence of discrete parts required by language, without destroying its essence? This is the challenge all dreamers face in trying to communicate their world. I face the same challenge in writing this book. How can my words successfully begin to describe the holistic experience of dreaming?

Many mystics who live in the imaginal world describe for us how it is utterly beyond their powers to convey in words what happens in the ecstatic moment of communion with the divine. Perhaps closer to the voice we are seeking is the voice used by the poets. Shakespeare puts an almost technically detailed description of how this imaginal world works, into the mouth of Theseus, the only dispassionate, rational character in *A Midsummer Night's Dream*:

The poet's eye, in fine frenzy rolling,
Doth glance from heaven to earth, from earth to heaven;
And as imagination bodies forth
The forms of things unknown, the poet's pen
Turns them to shapes and gives to airy nothing
A local habitation and a name.

Poets flourish at precisely this juncture between the imaginal and the verbal. To them the dream world is primal; verbal language is the servant of the dream. For the poet, living movements of the imaginal body give rise to words as the earth gives rise to a fountain of life. The words of the imaginal body don't necessarily follow each other in a rational sequence as they would in an intellectual argument. In poetry there are leaps, amazing juxtapositions, shocking associations.

Closer still to the imaginal world are ancient languages such as Hebrew and Sanskrit. Unlike modern languages which are a step removed from direct experiencing, Hebrew and Sanskrit have stayed close to the primal sounds and movements of what they are trying to convey. Their words and signs (alphabets such as the ancient Egyptian hieroglyphic) are transliterations of recurring, and therefore recognizable, body experiences.

THERE IS NO UNCONSCIOUS

Dreaming is a process that feeds upon itself. A person who wishes to start this process must catch the tail of the beast, the "Leviathan" from Hebrew lore that hides at the bottom of the ocean (the ocean in question being the subconscious), and ". . . makes a path to shine after him" (Job 42:24). The beast is the great body of knowledge in us that lies submerged beyond our conscious thoughts. *Can we learn to tap this body of knowledge?*

The word "unconscious" is a misnomer that has been bandied about for far too long, creating a false thought-form. Are we to accept that two-thirds of ourselves are forever sunk in the cold waters of the unknowable? Or can we, like the great Leviathan, come to the surface and tip over, exposing our hidden parts?

If we persevere in examining the subconscious carefully, we will see that it *does* reveal its secrets. If we dare to ask a question of our subconscious, we will be granted an answer. Therefore, for the sake of truth, let's agree to ban the word "unconscious" from this book and from our vocabulary. Instead, we will use the word "subconscious."

To inquire about the subconscious is the first step in this journey we have undertaken together. But what do we inquire about, since what we are seeking is hidden? How do we catch the tail of the beast? Where do we start?

TWO DIFFERENT REALITIES

Let's first clear the way by getting rid of a problem that our conscious mind has constructed for us: the myth that reality, defined as measurable, verifiable, repeatable phenomena, is the only reality there is. The conscious mind, caught in its own powerful thrust to provide irrefutable proofs for the nature of all things, has thrown out the baby with the bathwater.

Disowning its twin sibling which is the imaginal mind, the conscious mind has fed upon its ability to "know" reality. For four centuries and more it has gloried in measuring, verifying, and proving what it knows. A huge cultural ego has grown around this ability to fix knowledge.

In the words of this theorizing ego: What cannot be proven is not true, what is not verifiable does not exist. The mathematical, causal, delimited world is the *only* certain and grounded truth, all other phenomena are phantasmagoria of our minds unless proven otherwise.

This way of thinking is very seductive, as it greatly reduces the uncertainties we face and allows us to believe that we control our environment. This way of thinking has provided the basis for extraordinary technical achievements and discoveries about the physical world, and we are not here to deny its obvious validity. But pinning down a captured butterfly, while saving it for our inspection, also kills it. Rather, we would like to make a commonsense plea for the right to describe and study the *imaginal* world using *that* world's categories and priorities.

OTHERWORLDLY EXPERIENCES

What do we make of the countless otherworldly and elusive experiences people report that do not fit in with our verifiable world? It seems none of us are completely immune to such events, yet few of us will readily admit to having experienced them. However, when prompted, it is amazing how many people will talk of seeing ghosts, dead relatives that came back, guides, and angelic visitors.

They'll talk of mirrors exploding for no known reason, objects disappearing and reappearing a few days later; they have had dreams that came true, double visions of the real world and another world superimposed, or an instant recognition of truths that changed their lives.

Recently, I had dinner with a neighbor who told me that several times she had seen what she described as a Rembrandt-like figure appearing at the foot of her bed. "He was real, I saw him exactly as I see you! He stood there and looked at me intently, I felt he wanted to tell me something. I was scared to death!" Are all these people having delusions? Are they projecting their fantasies onto the real world? Or are they picking up on actual phenomena out there?

Strange perceptions, fantasies, hallucinations, eerie sounds, smells or tastes, goose bumps and other kinesthetic reactions, dreams, daydreams, visions, déjà-vu, clairvoyance, telepathy, sudden unfounded intuitions and certainties, non-causal happenings: the list is bewilderingly varied, yet I can volunteer a guess that 80 percent of the population has experienced at least one such phenomenon in their lives. It is also safe to assume that, like the lady with the Rembrandt-like visitor, most of us are scared to death by these phenomena that we don't understand.

Disbelief, embarrassment, and fear are the most common reasons why we shy away from giving permission to our minds to really examine these experiences. So let's create a working axiom, one that for the time being will help assuage the doubts (and embarrassment) of your left brain: *what cannot be proven is not necessarily untrue.*

This allows us to accept what we "see" while we yet lack the simple logical tools, or a paradigm, to prove it. As for fear, is it not there to teach us courage? Confronting mysteries may lead us on fascinating adventures we would otherwise miss if we were to give in to our fear.

TWO "REAL" WORLDS

Therefore, can we agree that the messages of both the objective left brain and the subjective right brain are "real" in different ways? Driving around a curve on a small dirt road in Massachusetts, I bumped into a polar bear. He was real! I saw him! He stood in the middle of the road staring at me, but in objective reality, well, he was not there, he existed only as a vision. My left brain knew for certain there are no polar bears in Massachusetts. Did my vision of the bear have any meaning?

For my right brain it did; there was something shockingly powerful about the hulky, silent bear that I couldn't ignore. It made me change the way I was conducting my life at that time. Otherworldly phenomena have a way of doing that. They shake us up, as surely as coming close to being run over by a truck will shake us up in real life.

Night dreams have that power, too. For instance, you have a dream that an intruder is breaking into your house, you sit up terrified, you shake your companion awake, you look all over the house to make sure no one *has* broken in. Is the dream real? Definitely, you really *felt* fear at the idea that someone had broken into your house. But is it a reality? No, in so far as you know, for you have just checked all the windows and doors and every room. Therefore, as no one actually broke into your house, does your dream mean anything?

Does it mean that someone *will* break in, and the dream is a warning? Or that, metaphorically speaking, you are being invaded, and therefore should examine your daily life to see who or what you are experiencing as an invasion?

Dream images can be many different things. Precisely because of this, some modern researchers have called all dream images "mind garbage." But this is like telling you to throw out all your mail because *some* of it is useless to you. If you continue to read this book, you will soon realize that consigning your dream images to the garbage is seldom the wisest way to deal with them.

Suppose I put my hand on my heart and say to you, "I have a pain here." You will not know if my pain is emotional or if I have heartburn. Only the context can tell you that or, if you don't know the context, by asking me a direct question about my pain.

It is the same with dream images. If I dream that I put my hand on my heart and the next morning I wake up with heartburn, I know that my pain is physical and the meaning of my dream image is made clear.

On this level, assigning a meaning to a dream depends on how closely the dream images are connected to the "real" world. As long as I am able to easily verify connections between reality and my dream images by assigning a meaning to them, my waking verbal self remains comfortably in control, and therefore separate from the world of dreamers.

But what if I, like the unfortunate people in asylums, can no longer tell the difference between dreams and reality?

NIGHT DREAMS ARE MORE ACCEPTABLE

Remember the original question that came up when the scientist interviewed the druid: What is the difference between dreams that come to us when we are asleep and *conscious* dreaming? One answer is that night dreams are more acceptable. No one thinks it's crazy to have a dream while asleep. Some people dream effusively and no one thinks to accuse *them* of being abnormal.

But the time that our dreams occur, whether night or day, does not define what dreaming is or is not; it is simply convenient for us to act as though it did. By saying that dreaming only happens at night when we are asleep we have created a clear separation between the outside world and the dream world. It helps us to feel more secure if our sleeping world doesn't bleed into our waking world. We can hold onto what we think is stable: the outside world. We cling to our supposed ability to distinguish the separation, for we are convinced our safety depends on our being able to see reality as it is.

Of course, our many problems come from the fact that few, if any, of us are able to "see reality as it is," simply because the boundary between the two worlds is far less well-defined than we would like to think.

The separation we create is artificial, but very potent. "This is fantasy, this is reality," we say and, in so doing, we feel like little children swaddled against the great void. Our bodies thus shielded, we can contemplate the vast world beyond us and the vast world inside of us with a semblance of surety on both sides.

WHAT STANDS BETWEEN THE TWO WORLDS?

Understand, then, that the true juncture between the two worlds is the body. This is where you start. *Trust your body.* In the womb, enclosed, turned in upon itself, your body dreams. At birth, the body is thrust outward: eyes meet light, skin touches objects, and ears hear the sharp sounds of life that, in the womb, were muffled by the cushioning ocean of amniotic fluid.

In other words, your sensations are the pathways in *both* directions, to the concrete *and* to the dream world. The senses act as doors that swing in or out at will.

I was once having dinner with a new friend, an established scientist. In our conversation, I started telling him about the swinging doors of the senses when suddenly he got up and said he didn't want to be friends with someone who believed such nonsense. But, since he has a body, what *he* calls nonsense is *in him* too.

If you have a pain and turn your eyes in to the pain, you will be able to describe it. It is hot, wet, cold, inflamed, red, dull, etc. If you continue to look at it, you might actually "see" images or hear sounds. These, too, tell you about your pain. *Experience always talks to us in the language of the senses.*

The inner world of the right brain is three-dimensional. In it, as in the outer world, we operate with all of our senses: we see, hear, smell, taste, and even touch. Have you ever had a passionate sexual encounter in a night dream that led to an actual physical discharge? The pleasure was so vivid that your body responded physically, and appropriately, to the dream stimulation.

Dreaming of a physical activity in the night dream—running the marathon, for example—is not the same as actually running the marathon. In the outer world you are bound by the rules of the outer world and suffer the effects of its limitations: exhaustion, thirst, heat, and pain—while in your dream you run effortlessly.

But if you check your legs the next morning, you'll probably discover that your muscles feel as tired as they would after a tough workout. The images from your dreams have induced micro-movements in your muscles. This, by the way, is the basis of all sport visualization. The dream images dialogue with your body, stimulating muscle response.

Dream acts on the physical world. The images may be "fantasy," but their effects are real. Imagination affects the physical, and vice-versa. The two worlds interact through the body. The way a great band of nerve fibers, the corpus callosum, connects your right and left brain hemispheres, your body also connects your inner dream world with the outside physical world.

Your body is the boundary and the link. Being securely grounded in your body, with a strong habit of paying attention to the messages your senses give you, maintains your access to both worlds while, at the same time, safeguarding you from the danger of losing yourself in either.

PAYING ATTENTION TO YOUR SENSATIONS

By paying attention to your sensations, you catch the tail of the beast. Staying grounded in the present and becoming skillful at listening to what your body's senses are telling you is the first step in your training as a dreamer.

Imagine this scenario: you meet someone, and simultaneously you "see" that the room has darkened. Your next step is to immediately pay attention to your body; note whether or not your solar plexus is tensing. And how is your breathing? Has it become shallow? The darkening of the room expresses a subjective impression: call it an intuition.

In this example, your "intuition" is a signal that your waking dream self has decided to take a hand in what is going on. You know that, except for your perception of it, the room didn't actually darken, but still, what you "saw" is telling you something about the real world out there. It is telling you about your reaction to the person you have just met. Your task now is to try to find the reason for what you have experienced.

Begin your search by trying to see if your body was in a completely clear state at the time the event occurred. By that I mean, was it acting as an *impersonal* radar when it picked up signals from the other person? Or were you projecting a feeling from your memory bank onto this person?

For instance, if this person happened to resemble someone you dislike, it's possible that an unpleasant memory was behind the darkening of the room. Recognizing this possibility, you have to ask yourself the question: Is my reaction a fallacy? Am I imagining something about this person that is not true?

It is at this point that most people bow out because they feel they can't tell the difference between their projections and their dreaming. It is simply easier for them to reject the world of images as mere falsehood and fantasy. They leave their causal minds in control and, once again, pass up the riches that might have been theirs had they accepted what their dreaming mind was saying.

Like Perceval (the hero of the Grail romances) who, having been granted a vision of the Holy Grail in the castle of the mysterious Fisher King, neglects to inquire about the vision's meaning and applicability and, as a result, loses his faith in the numinous and in God, these people who bow out lose inestimable treasures by not asking questions when confronted with a dream occurrence.

TRUE DREAMING VERSUS PROJECTIONS

Instead of bowing out, is there a dependable way to bring clarity to our search for the meaning inherent in our dream experiences? What will help the dreamer sift out his false projections so that he can begin to become a *true* dreamer? Becoming a true dreamer is the main goal of the teachings described in this book, as these teachings can lead you to an entirely new way to live your dreams.

I have broken the teachings down into twelve consecutive tasks. By the time you reach the last task you should feel that you can easily distinguish true inner vision from mere projections or fantasies.

To become a dreamer, seer, visionary, or even a prophet, you must go on a journey to the center of your imaginal mind, as did the sages of old.

You will begin this journey in chapter 1 ("Pattern and Perception") by learning to observe how you tend to gravitate towards certain patterns while ignoring others, thereby limiting "your reality." Although you may believe that "your reality" is the only reality out there, you are in fact *dreaming* your own particular brand of it. Will you stay stuck in your same old box or can you enlarge your perspective and shift your point of view to encompass more of the reality that is potentially available to you?

In chapter 2 ("The STOP! Game – Setting Up Your Life Plan"), you will see how your inner vision of what is possible and available to you is clouded by your thwarted instincts, desires, expectations, claims, etc., which further contributes to narrowing the vision of your reality.

How does this work? We mostly operate in the realm of instincts and emotions. Emotions are *reactions* to thwarted instincts. To reach the realm of *response*, which allows you to be open to the world as opposed to being reactive to it, you must begin the process of sorting out your instincts from your reactions. This will allow you to begin setting up what I call the "Life Plan," which is a map of how you are presently behaving versus how you would prefer to behave in the future.

You start the process by playing the STOP! game, which teaches you to mimic life by deliberately choosing to stop your untoward desires as they begin to manifest. You will do this, not to punish yourself, but to redirect your energy into channels that are more conducive to your growth and happiness.

In chapter 3 ("Paying Attention to Your Dreams") you will find out how your emotions and thwarted desires play out in your dream time. Most of you have conveniently lost the ability to remember your dreams, because their clouded and muddied messages are not pleasant to contemplate. You drown your nightmares, recurring dreams, and busy dreams in a flurry of daytime activity.

To clear the mirror of your muddied emotions, which will allow "true dreaming" to appear, it is important that you first train yourself to remember your dreams, even if they are repugnant to you. How you will conquer your hidden resistance, how you will train yourself to remember, and what you will do with your dreams once you remember them is part of this third task.

In chapter 4 ("Interacting with the Dream"), instead of ignoring the impact of your dream images, you will learn to face the challenges they present. This requires a shift in attitude. Taking your dreams seriously is the first step in becoming a committed dreamer; as a committed dreamer you will be able to enlist your imagination as a powerful tool in achieving your Life Plan. As a child, you used to play and invent, and thus you educated yourself to face the challenges of this world. Here you are going to apply those same rules of creativity and learn the fun of interacting playfully with your dreams.

So far you have dealt with dreaming in your waking state. In chapter 5 ("Reversing") you will learn to come closer to the dream world, which is the mirror image—or reverse—of your daytime world. By consciously adopting the reverse, or dreaming point of view, at the moment you are falling asleep, you will learn to discover things about yourself that only the dream world can show you.

The act of Reversing is a dreaming maneuver that shifts you out of your habitual forwardness into another, new, viewpoint which will encourage you to look at how the dreaming world responds to what is happening in your daytime world. You will learn that your dream images are not the mawkish fare they are often depicted to be, but powerful, sometimes shocking, ever-impacting truths that may very well jolt you out of your complacence and into a better place.

In chapter 6 ("Returning to Your Senses") you will recognize how difficult it is to conquer your instinctual patterns and to trick yourself out of the limitations of your physicality. How, for instance, do you become awake *and* conscious in your sleep? Amazingly, it is only when pain prompts you and you travel back in through the doorways of your senses, i.e., when you utilize your physicality in a *conscious* and precise way, that you will be able to become awake and aware in your *subconscious* dreaming world.

But why rely only on night dreams when you can plunge directly and instantly into the *source* of your dreaming and be rewarded with your experiencing, "dreaming mind's" point of view? Dreaming happens at every moment, for you are experiencing life at every moment. To have continuous access to your dreaming, you must train yourself to consciously plunge, over and over again, into the *source* of your dreaming.

In chapter 7 ("Practicing Life's Quickening Exercises") you will start practicing exercises (short inductions which have been constructed according to specific laws of the Imagination, which I'll discuss), that will trigger in you, the dreamer, the tension, jolt, or thrill of experiencing necessary to plummet you into the immediacy and freshness of the source.

If the aim of the Guided Exercises and the dream recall was to simply satisfy a vicarious curiosity, your practice would soon lose its dynamism. In chapter 8 ("Intent and Dreaming") you will learn that your dreaming must be pro-active in firing your will to bring into manifestation what you have dreamt. *Kavanah* (your will or "intent") is your dream's sibling. Without kavanah, your dreaming would become stagnant.

Dreaming needs to be propelled into reality and kavanah is the fire which does that. Its movement is fuelled, not by the sheer force of will, not by nightmares, recurring dreams, or busy dreams, not even by the clear dream, but by what is called the "great dream" (which occurs in the nighttime) or the "prophetic vision" (which occurs in the daytime) that arises from the very source of feeling.

Even if you are being propelled forward by a great dream or a prophetic vision and are thus compelled to accomplish your Life Plan, there are times when the wind drops and the energy goes out of your sails. You find yourself at loose ends, depressed, anxious, or in a morass of indecision. To cut the Gordian knot of your indecision, in chapter 9 ("The Waking Dream") you are going to learn to allow yourself to sink below your confusion, into the dreaming world where you will freely move about. From this, your kavanah, if not your answer itself, will re-emerge in the free unfolding of images. This process is called "Waking Dream."

Again and again you may find yourself, as we all do at one time or another, stymied by old patterns, buffeted by old emotions, or caught in old stories. Until you are able to break your negative emotional chain, link by link, you will be governed by images of your past.

At some point, however, even your great dreams, prophetic visions, and experiences of the Waking Dream may not be able to help you to break away from your past. In chapter 10 ("Changing the Past") you will learn practices specifically designed to help you change your emotional connections to the past. These dreaming techniques are called "Reversing the Past."

In chapter 11 ("The Master Game: Perfecting the Life Plan") you are ready to play the master game and to perfect your Life Plan. To finally and definitely transmute your nightmares and busy dreams into great dreams you must anchor yourself in feeling, not in emotion. This is work that must be continually perfected in order to avoid slipping back into old habits, in the same way that you must constantly fight gravity in order to avoid slumping.

Shifting from *reactivity* to *feeling* is done progressively, because the body is a creature of habit. In this chapter, you will learn to create a "dreaming kavanah" by chanting words on a three-note scale. This ancient practice is called "Words."

Chapter 12 ("Return to Oneness") will show you how to integrate, into your daily life, the practices you have learned in this book. You will also learn to use your imbalances to propel yourself further into the *feeling* zone. Balance is only of the moment, but each time you reach it you know you have reached above your nature to what the French call "Surnature." If you do this often enough, you will anchor yourself in the heartland.

When this happens your dreaming becomes clearer, lighter, and brighter. Eventually, your dreaming becomes all light. Light is the reward that your practice will bring you, as well as a sense of peace, harmony, love, and joy. At this point, whatever you do will become effortless as your two minds—your conscious mind and your dreaming mind—dance together, weaving a life that is richer and more abundant than you ever could have envisioned it would be.

True dreaming calls for rigorous training and demands determination and dedication of its devotees. At first, your dreams will be full of false projections, because your needs, expectations, claims, hopes, and fears are running the show. To use the teachings to clear your dreams, to hone your imagination until "True Imagination" shines through, is the goal of our quest.

Many knights and ladies have left their secure homes and plunged into the magical realm of their illusions, fantasies, and false projections. Like Odysseus' men who, on their journey back home, were seduced and then turned into pigs by the enchantress Circe, these present-day seekers must disarm the dangers they face by determining when these visions are nothing more than mere aspects of themselves (which can manifest in multi-faceted ways, for instance, as alluring damsels, wind-mills, dangerous beasts, or beckoning forests).

Victory over our illusions and projections comes when we are able to distinguish, in our bodies, the difference in sensation between our surface reactions and our true intuitive feelings. In thus securing our imagination to the movements of the body, we clear our inner screen to reflect the wisdom that is waiting to shine through. This is where the great power of dreaming comes into our hands.

ONE

Pattern and Perception

"Who has measured the waters in the hollow of his hand,
Marked off the heavens with a span,
Enclosed the dust of the earth in a measure,
Weighed the mountains in scales
And the hills in balance?"

ISAIAH 40:12

We live in a world made recognizable through patterns and forms and, should they disappear, this world would become lost to us. We find both our pleasure and our pain in patterns and forms and have a love/hate relationship with them. And while we would feel totally naked and vulnerable without a sense of boundaries (left brain), at the same time we long to escape their imprisonment (right brain).

Haven't we all struggled to break the forms? To be free of them for just one moment? To return back, in our mind's eye, to the nothingness before the beginning? It is a quasi-impossible task, for the left brain's vice-like hold on us is very powerful.

Yet every day of our lives we witness such a moment, as the vanishing sun returns shapes to the darkness from whence they came. Dusk is the sacred time given to us to witness the disappearance of forms, followed by dawn, the wondrous moment when shapes miraculously reappear.

The manner in which we experience these privileged moments affects our bodies, our emotions. It also may reveal to us the secret of how we can teach ourselves to switch back and forth at will between our two brains, between stability (left brain) and freedom (right brain), those two all-important elements in the growth of our minds and personalities.

If we discount sleep, the closest we can come to consciously experiencing no pattern, no form, is by beholding chaos: a wild, disordered exuberance or an endless monotony that cancels out single determinants. Such is the abundance of the Amazon Jungle as seen from a plane, or a crowd so vast it is like an ocean, or a desert of yellow sand baking in the scorching sun, or a prison cell whose blank walls give no inkling of the passage of time.

If you have ever felt unnerved by riotous abundance, or misplaced your ability to recognize some familiar shape you can latch onto, you will know how the body loses itself. How that fear, the awe of "no-thing," dissolves our boundaries. We need shape to shape ourselves. Yet we also need a vacation away from shape to allow ourselves, when we return, a larger gamut of choices within the patterned tapestry of this world.

Once, as I was watching my son run screeching with glee into a flock of seagulls, the world cancelled out: no form, no light, no me! It was a total experience. When I could see again, there was my son on a wharf, the seagulls swirling above him. I felt complete.

For years I had tried to blink away the world and thus it was an incredible relief to shut off pattern for even that one instant. The event confirmed my certainty that life is sustained by our search for pattern. The counterpoint to this, and the simple secret to breaking away from pattern and form, is a place in life for empty space. As much as we need shape, we need the pause away from shape, which only the oblivion of sleep or the airy emptiness of the right brain can provide.

* * *

STRANGE ATTRACTORS

We are so driven to find meaning in the world that, when we are confronted with the chaotic profusion of nature, we instinctively search out clusters of color, finding patterns in a screen of leaves, or in the swirls and eddies of a stream, or in clouds in the sky. We assign to a stranger on the street a fleeting resemblance to a friend. We find strange echoes from the past in the diffused light of a room at sunset.

Although chance events may push us uncontrollably in directions we haven't chosen, we look for *and find* a subtle order in the changes, and this order, when we have placed it, restores meaning to our lives. *We can sustain some chaos, but pattern grounds our lives.* Without pattern, life ceases to make sense—we get sick, we go mad, we may even die.

How do we explain our predilections? Despite the absence of conscious choice, there appears to be an overall pattern to our search for individual patterns. Without asking our permission, the brain seems to gravitate towards certain patterns while ignoring others.

In chaos theory the term for objects that show this dynamic of predilection is "strange attractors." What is the origin of these strange attractors that accounts for, but does not explain, the great variety found in people's tastes and life patterns? I am attracted to shimmering colors of gold and green, to mystical texts, and brilliant men. My friend loves the stock market, wears only black, and likes muscular men.

Nonetheless, putting these differences in taste aside, we are friends, each of us seeing something in the other that attracts us to one another. This resonance of affection is perhaps the strongest, most important strange attractor of all. It is the pattern, sometimes small and barely perceived, at other times so great it overwhelms most of our consciousness, that ultimately guides everyone's life. Is affection self-similarity making itself known through the bias of another?

MIND AND CREATION

We could say that our mind exteriorizes itself. It recognizes itself outside, in the patterns of the created world, and reflects back to itself, inside, those patterns which best reflect its being. This quest for self-similarity progresses to incorporate ever-expanding coils of a spiraling web of understanding.

The curious mind, observing the world and itself, probes further, looking for what it is by looking at what its world is like. The mind is insatiable in its search for meaningful patterns, which Kabbalah calls *partzufim,* or "faces" of God. And yet, paradoxically, when Man, having reached beyond the created world to his ultimate other, comes face to face with the unknowable, the mystery, God, and sees they are the same, two dissolve into One. Pattern, and with it duality, disappears. Which is why, when we read the story of the creation of the world in the Bible, we see that on the seventh day, after God (out of "affection," i.e., from looking for Himself) creates Man "in His Image," there is a pause (all forms having dissolved into unity) before a new beginning.

Only in the empty space of a pause can a new creation arise and, with it, the leap necessary to our uncovering of new, strange attractors.

WE DREAM OUR REALITY

Once you understand that, in *perceiving* your world you *create* it, you are then ready to understand how *what* you are attracted to defines the way you see the world and yourself. *You make the world fit into the parameters of your strange attractors.* Since you gravitate only towards certain configurations and ignore others, your worldview is essentially limited and your beliefs about your possibilities are also restricted.

Pattern, by definition, has boundaries and shape. We could say that you are dreaming your reality. But your dream is hemmed in by what you choose to focus on. Only when you look beyond the dream you are caught in can you imagine a new reality.

Eventually your dream may enlarge to include the whole world and, beyond that, touch "no-thingness." But then you could lose yourself! That is the paradox you will encounter as you become a true dreamer: to be able to experience the lightness and freedom beyond pattern and yet remain grounded in your earthly body! But wait, you have a long way to go before you face that dilemma. It will be your last task; one that you will encounter in the last chapter of this book.

As it is, your first task of learning to recognize your strange attractors is difficult enough. Let's begin by asking: What do you naturally gravitate toward? An easier way to think about this is: What are your interests? Start there.

Identifying Your Strange Attractors

Take a sheet of paper and write down a list of all your interests. When you have done that (take your time, giving yourself at least three days), look at your list. Then sit down in an armchair with your arms and legs uncrossed. Close your eyes, breathe out slowly three times and count backwards from three to one, seeing the numbers in your mind. Then ask yourself: What

are the glaring omissions? What am I not allowing myself to be attracted to? Don't try to think about this, instead allow patterns and images to surface in your mind. Give names to the images. Breathe out and open your eyes. List the names of those images in a separate column.

Remember that only that towards which you gravitate becomes a reality for you. The rest is mainly lost to you. Does this mean you are determined by the strange attractors in your brain, that your genetic make-up is responsible for the choices you make? Can you change or modify, in part, your strange attractors, thereby giving yourself choices in defining your reality? The answer to all these questions is "yes."

By simply becoming aware of your strange attractors you begin the process of enlarging your dream, and therefore your possibilities. By asking yourself what you are missing, you are opening yourself up to the prospect of new realities.

The Bible creation myth tells us we are the manifest reality of God. Since we are the dream of God, we *are* God, and therefore co-creators in the world's creation. But we get caught in the unpacking of the dream and get bogged down in realities that obscure the greater reality.

We have the freedom to change our realities to reflect more and more of the total reality that *is* God. (I use the word "God" to reflect the vocabulary of the Bible myth, but feel free to substitute the word that best suits your beliefs and philosophy.)

Our participation is essential in allowing us to expand our vision. Where do we start? We start by understanding more about the mechanism that gets us caught in fixed, stagnant configurations.

* * *

WE ARE INFORMED BY FORM

The English language instructs us on how things are. It tells us we are "in-formed." Our sensations in-form us. Those taste buds, eardrums, cilia (enabling our sense of smell), rods and cones (enabling our sense of sight), subcutaneous receptors and tactile hairs (enabling our sense of touch) vibrate locally, sending their messages via nerve ways to the brain. This localized information comes from molecular shapes touching the cilia in our nose cavities, or from wave patterns carried by the atmosphere setting our eardrums in motion, or from light vibrations impacting our retinas.

Always we are informed by form, whether the form is palpable or not. The wind informs us of its presence by the direction and amplitude of its voice; by the motions it imposes on leaves, hats, or flags; by its touch—light or strong, wet or dry, cold or warm—on our bodies. Yet the wind is invisible. We are wired to pick up and to recognize pattern.

Certain patterns give us color, others scent, others sound or texture, temperature, or shape. Each sense receptor is specialized to receive only one kind of stimulation and is shut off from all other forms of stimulation.

We can say that sensations discriminate. For example, on the skin there are different receptors for light pressure, for deep stimulation, for warmth, for cold, for pain. We group all these receptors under the general "sense" called touch.

Taste, for instance, is not only located in the taste buds of our tongue. Taste disappears if we lose our sense of smell. Without smell, touch, texture, and temperature, there is no taste. In other words, what we call "taste" is not a simple sensory experience—each element sensed separately—but an organized experience manifesting as a synergy of all the sense stimuli which have been activated in the process of our experiencing it. This organized experience is called *perception*.

Imagine that *sensations* are the dots on your television screen while *perception* is the total, defined image that you accept as the television picture. In other words, you deconstruct and reconstruct a pattern in the process of perceiving it.

TRICKS OF PERCEPTION

Let us for the moment define perception as the brain's way of reconstructing the outside. Is perception accurate? Have you ever seen the film *Rashomon*, directed by Akira Kurosawa, the great Japanese filmmaker? It recounts the story of a rape and murder as seen through the eyes of four witnesses.

Each story, as you may have guessed, is different. Where is the truth? From the point of view of the perceiver, what he or she "sees" is the truth. But think of it this way: your perception is limited by your physical location. You saw this car burn a red light, but another witness, standing on the other side of the street, thinks the driver passed through the light when it was yellow. Who is telling the truth? Well, both of course (unless one is lying). But what is The Truth?

When there are discrepancies, is it the fault of perception or of our interpretation of the entire perceptual picture on our inner screen? We know that, in the act of translation from the sensory stimuli to the brain, there is a brief period, from 100 to 200 milliseconds at most, during which a disruption of the unhindered perception can occur. As they say, a funny thing can happen on the way to the forum.

For instance, you were knocked down by a car once, so this now "colors" your perception; you are not so tolerant of drivers whizzing through yellow lights. Due to your acquired expectation that all drivers are a danger to pedestrians, you might actually "see" (in good faith, of course), the driver burn the red light.

Perception or, to be more exact, the act of translating to yourself the perceptual totality reflected on your inner screen, is more fluid and thus more subject to errors during translation and adjustment than we realize. It is also more fixed than we think. Remember the lyrics of the song that Pete Seeger sings, *Little Boxes, Little Boxes*? "And they're all made out of ticky-tacky, and they all look just the same." Because of your fixed idea about drivers, you pick up certain details and omit others in order to fit this particular driver into *your* "little box" called "dangerous driver."

PERCEPTION AS THE MIRROR

Unadulterated perception, on the other hand, is like a mirror, a reflective empty space. In the kabbalistic literature, Adam HaKadmon, the first man, had, before his fall from grace, a body as large as the universe, and it was totally transparent. When God looked into His creation He saw, not the shapes of His creation, but the clear pool of His own being. For God, there was no distortion of the mirror.

> *I am silver and exact. I have no preconceptions.*
> *Whatever I see I swallow immediately*
> *Just as it is, unmisted by love or dislike.*

I am not cruel, only truthful—
the eye of a little god, four-cornered.
"MIRROR" 1961, SYLVIA PLATH

But for Man, the story played itself out differently. In Adam and Eve's fall from their pristine state, their mirror, their hitherto transparent body, became abhorrent to them, for now they could distinguish between two warring patterns: good and evil. Caught in their awareness of the new shape of things, a duality which already constituted both their pleasure and their pain, they felt ashamed and tried to hide from God. God in His compassion gave them skins woven from the threads of their animal nature, their guilt, fear, and desire, to cover what had become the unbearable truth of their pure perception.

Now I am a lake. A woman bends over me,
Searching my reaches for what she really is.
Then she turns to those liars, the candles or the moon.
I see her back, and reflect it faithfully.
She rewards me with tears and an agitation of hands.
I am important to her. She comes and goes.
Each morning it is her face that replaces the darkness.
In me she has drowned a young girl, and in me an old woman
Rises toward her day after day, like a terrible fish.
"MIRROR" 1961, SYLVIA PLATH

What we see reflected in the mirror may not be what we *want* to see. We may be tempted to adulterate its message to fit in with our needs or our desires. Yet this has nothing to do with the mirror. We (that part of our brain that translates the pure perception into meaning) are the ones who, fearing the truth, tinker with its message. The mirror remains the same, reflecting faithfully what is out there or, though less commonly realized, what is within.

But what *is* within? The question is intrinsic to the world of imagination. How can we perceive the inner world if it doesn't exist concretely? How can something not objectified be reflected back into our perceptual mirror? *Let us postulate that our imagination is the unfathomable in a dialogue with the known, dreaming a language rising out*

of an abyss of mystery to the surface of our perceptual mirror in
response to the manifest world.

To start this dialogue we can begin by visualizing our inner mirror.
We can imagine it square, as did Sylvia Plath in the poem above, or we
can see it as spherical, like the human eye. It reflects information from
both worlds—within and without—on its spherical surface. Or you can
imagine it as a two-sided coin with a different picture on each face.
Either way, it receives and reflects without preconceptions.

To reach its clear depths we must either shock our distorting selves
totally out of the way, thus gaining instantaneous insight into the truth,
(this is further elaborated on in chapter 7), or systematically clear each
one of the disruptions that stand in our way.

GENETIC CAUSES OF
PERCEPTUAL DISRUPTION

Perceptual disruptions of the outer world can be classified into two
groups: the genetic and the environmental.

The most powerful and constant disruption to pure perception is
our genetic make-up. It is our genetic background which partly determines our strange attractors. How does this work? Imagine you are
born color-blind. This anomaly will have an impact on your life. You
won't be very good at picking strawberries in the field since you aren't
able to quickly distinguish between the green leaves and the red fruit.
You probably won't find work in fashion or interior design, either.

Our shape, the morphology of our body, our physical pre-dispositions
(strong lungs, weak spine, nervous condition, etc.), will set our lives on a
course that is somewhat ordained. We could say that our antecedents com-
bine to create a vehicle that is wired to comfortably perform only certain,
specified functions. The vehicle can be extremely complex, have a large
field of functions, and be adaptable to changes. Yet it will have limits.

Take a Ferrari. It is designed to move in a fast and powerful way.
At the same time, it is not made to transport a family of five, plus the
dog. A Jeep Cherokee, on the other hand, accommodates the family, but
has to give up the fast maneuverability of a Ferrari. The family of five
plus the dog are the strange attractors that the Jeep Cherokee draws to
itself. They are its reality.

What can we do about our genetic make-up? Does it determine us, like the Jeep Cherokee, to a certain reality? The answer to this is a qual-ified "yes." The destiny of man is to fully embody the potential offered by the genetic structure that is given to him. Each human being incarnates to fulfill that purpose. But human beings respond to their environment, they have the power of choice, and they function on many different levels.

In most of us, some of these levels will remain dormant, others we will be forced to put to use by outside circumstance, still others we can choose to develop or not. For example, you have musical abilities, yet you never developed them. Instead you became a mathematician.

There is a lot more flexibility within our genetic structure than we may imagine. The message is that we don't need to confine ourselves to narrow limits. New strange attractors, like so many Sleeping Beauties, are waiting to be awakened by our kiss. Discovering our dormant genetic gifts is all about fun and freedom.

ENVIRONMENTAL DISRUPTIONS

More difficult to deal with than genetic endowments are the environ-mental restraints which have conditioned us, through repeated pro-gramming from the outside, to a narrowed perspective on life. This conditioning is there from the beginning of life.

Imagine two infants and their mothers. As soon as the first one cries, his mother picks him up, checks him to see what he needs, and sets out to gratify his desires as quickly as she can. When the other infant cries, her mother lets her exhaust herself until she stops or cries herself to sleep.

During their infancy each of these two children is taught to expect a different world. The stage has been set for them. The first child will resonate to intimacy and trustful connections, the other to loneliness and betrayal. Both children will believe that their own world is the true reality, unless they are jolted out of their expectations and made to res-onate to something different.

The second child is now a grown woman. Her expectations are poor, the range of her strange attractors impoverished, and she is pres-sured by her conditioning to gravitate towards men who will treat her like her mother did. She has been taught to expect people to ignore her emotional needs. When this happens it confirms her view of reality: her expectations have proven to be correct.

What she doesn't see is that she herself has created her own proof.

She has limited her reality to what she expects to see. In the grip of her negative conditioning, she has to watch her friends get married, while she just gets older. When she meets a man at a party and her first impression is negative, she ignores it. She wants this man to be Mister Right. She thus proceeds to distort her perception to fit her desire.

This vicious circle is hard to break, since the very patterns we need to see reflected in our perceptual mirror stand in the way of our being able to look into the mirror. We are being blinded by them but we do not know it. Our memories, conditioning, expediency, desires, hopes, expectations, claims, projections, language, illness, substance abuse, all these distort perception. As Jesus Christ reminds us, we easily identify the straw in another's eye, but we can't see the bigger splinter in our own. This will always be true if we can't find a way to clear our eye of the distortions that obscure it.

Here are two exercises to start you on the process of clearance.

The Blue Vase

Find a quiet place where you are not likely to be disturbed and where you can relax. Sit in an armchair with your arms and legs uncrossed. Close your eyes. Breathe out all that disturbs you, all that tires you, all that obscures you. Breathe it out as a light smoke (carbon dioxide) that is easily absorbed by the plant life around you. When your breath comes in on the inhalation, see it as blue as the radiant blue light from the sky, and filled with sunlight. See the blue golden light filling your nostrils, your mouth, your throat, and flowing down your back as a great river of light. See it filling your feet, your toes, and stretching out of your toes as long antennas of light. See the light circulating up your legs to fill your pelvis, see it rising up into your chest, flowing in and out of your heart until your heart becomes a glowing blue lamp. See the light flow down your arms like smaller rivers of light, fill your hands and fingers, stretch out of your fingers as long antennas of light. As you continue to breathe in the blue light, see the light continue to fill you. See it begin to radiate out of the articulations of your joints:

out of your ankles, knees, hips, shoulders, elbows, and wrists. See the light fill you until it radiates out of your skin in all directions. See yourself as a crystal vase filled with light and radiating light in all directions. Open your eyes, seeing yourself as the crystal vase radiating blue light in all directions. Then stop.

This exercise, you'll be surprised to hear, can be done in a minute, or in thirty seconds when you're practiced. Never take longer than a minute to do it. The Blue Vase is fantastic for giving you a boost of energy and is best practiced in the morning.

The Pendulum

Close your eyes. Breathe out three times slowly, counting from three to one. Picture the number one as tall, clear, and bright. Imagine a great crystal pendulum rhythmically swinging from left to right, right to left. Each time the pendulum swings to the right, it gathers, into a pile, the (environmental) disruptions in your life which have caused a narrowing of your choices. Try to identify each disruption as the pendulum pushes it onto the pile. When all have been gathered, breathe out. See the pendulum swing wide to the right and, swinging back to the left in a great sweep, transport the whole pile to the left. Breathe out and see the pendulum once again swing wide to the right and, swinging back to the left, knock the whole pile off to the left and out of the picture. Breathe out and open your eyes.

THE INNER WORLD

We have talked about perception in so far as it reflects the outer world. Let's look more closely now at what we mean by perception of the *inner world*. Is the inner world, as reflected in the perceptual mirror, a picture of our inside body? In other words, are we simply perceiving messages from inner physical stimuli? Or is the inner world an entity existing *beyond* the body?

As adults, we don't question our ability to apprehend the outer world for, in the process of growing up, we had to learn to distinguish shapes, colors, sounds, smells, and all the other clues that our senses naturally register and which come so easily to us now.

As infants, we knew naturally only how to dream and, in the process of growing from infancy to adulthood, we were pulled out of ourselves by exterior stimuli. Thus, as adults, we must be retrained to once again focus inward.

Perceiving the inner world requires a movement opposite to what we are most used to. Therefore it is necessary that we work consciously at the task of doing it. When we turn inward, what do we gaze at? Not form and pattern, but an empty space.

Remember, since the inner world is the reverse of the outer world, it takes us only a moment to pause from attending to the patterning of the outside world to allow us to perceive the inner world. I will point out here that, although we are looking inward, we are not looking *into* the body. (That is a different and localized form of "seeing" described in chapter 6.)

What we want to contemplate instead is a non-locality, an insubstantial, intangible, inside space. Instead of grasping for form and pattern, we tap into this empty space by the simple maneuver of looking in. Our active "seeing" brings light into the darkness and, in that light, we are gifted, as if by magic, with an unexpected play of configurations within the emptiness.

It is as if, on stretching our index finger to touch a blank wall, suddenly hitherto invisible letters pop forth. But try to fix them on the wall and they will just as quickly shift into another shape or vanish out of sight. In the inner world of a healthy individual, pattern doesn't imprison; instead it joyfully engages us in meaningful play; the meaningful play of the imagination.

But what then is "imagination"? Because its nature is so elusive, we can't pin it down to even an *approximate* definition. We have postulated that it is "the unknowable dialoguing with the known." Certainly, Imagination lives as if behind a veil, its power hidden in an impenetrable but pregnant ether. Is gazing on the empty space of the inner world our way in, our tunnel to an actual other world? Is dreaming a place, a "reality" we can visit, is it our Avalon behind the mists?

Can we pull off the trick of turning an octopus inside out by bringing real dreaming reality into our normal conscious reality? You will discover, as you continue reading this book, that all these things are possible.

Meanwhile, to return to our original question concerning inner perception, we want to point out that when our perception is turned inward it has no other function than to allow us to "see" Imagination, whose configurations, like fleeting clouds in an empty sky, float up in answer to our queries and vanish in the vast incommensurable inner light of our "seeing."

DISTORTIONS OF THE IMAGINATION

Is the inner face of the mirror subject to disruptions, too? Can the world of Imagination be manipulated, twisted, and distorted? Of course it can, just as our perception of the outer world can. Are these disruptions inherent to the world of Imagination? No, they owe their origins to the body.

By "body" I mean our frail human body with its fixed patterns and habits, needs, and emotions. It is these that latch onto the imagination to twist it and use it for daydreams and fantasies, those bastardized forms of dreaming that we recognize from the exhaustion they engender (whereas insight into pure imagination energizes us).

As an aside here, let us not confuse "daydreams" with what the French call *rêveries*. Rêveries take place in a relaxed, open-ended state of being that induces daytime dreaming, whereas daydreaming is led by our self-indulgent desires towards foregone conclusions.

For instance, you daydream that a man who has money and a house and is wonderfully handsome and sexy falls madly in love with you, sweeps you off your feet, and marries you. Of course, you live happily ever after. (Substitute "woman" as the subject of the daydream if you are a man.)

"Fantasies" disrupt the pure reflection of the inner world by feeding our needy, thwarted expectations. A fantasy could go something like this: "I'll break every finger of his hands, then every bone of his body one by one!" Or, "I'll die, then they'll see what they're missing," and you go on to fantasize about your funeral and your family's grief in fulsome detail.

Recognizing Daydreams and Fantasies

Spend the next week paying attention to the content of your daydreaming and of your fantasies. Observe them without judgment.

Paying attention to your daydreams and fantasies will show you where you are most blocked. For instance, your longing for companionship has you enthralled, or your anger is turning into an obsession. Thus are your strange attractors shaped and turned into realities that you may not relish but that you unfortunately become married to.

Learning to distinguish your daydreams and fantasies from pure imagination is the beginning of a process (described in following chapters) that will allow you to incorporate their images into your inner world's imaginary scenario in order to deal with them and then discharge them. The stagnant energies invested in maintaining these illusions are thus harvested by the imagination to create new, life-affirming configurations.

If we are normal and healthy, then we have a secure center inside ourselves from which to connect to the outside world. Like Adam, who named the animals (Genesis 2:19), we can name the different components of our world. Whatever disruptions we encounter in our perceptual processes, we are still able to see a world made congruent by patterns we recognize, patterns already named and fixed for our future reference.

The trouble is, the more we see the world this way, the more we tend to make the mistake of thinking this is the only way to see the world! We are self-referent creatures, we train ourselves as we go along, digging ourselves deeper into the groove we have chosen. Then we train our children to do the same.

Infants are born, like Adam HaKadmon (the first man), with a transparent inner body. Because any interest in the inner world is discouraged or ignored in children, their perception of it—so strong at first—quickly dwindles with the years.

But imagine something happening that shifts one's awareness, such as a terrible shock. For instance, your child is hurt, or you are diagnosed with cancer, or your lost lover returns to you. Fear or joy—either way, the shocking emotion flips your mirror. Suddenly you are looking at its other face.

In this newly discovered empty space of "no-thingness," imagination can float its short-lived but momentous signs. But is it necessary to wait for life's shocks in order to peer into its secrets? Each night there is a window of opportunity, a privileged moment when catching glimpses of that other world in its purity is possible. It makes much more sense to start your exploration of imagination there.

Seeing Hypnagogic Images

Tonight when you go to bed, allow yourself to relax completely. Close your eyes. Make sure you remain alert. Don't allow yourself any inner dialogue. Push away all thoughts by sweeping them out of your mind to the left. Remain in a restful, suspended "empty" watchful state. Soon you will "see" flashing colors, strange disconnected images, whole scenes in vivid detail. Under your closed eyelids these appear and disappear, just as quickly to be replaced by others. Don't try to hold on to them. Just watch. Soon you will naturally sink into sleep. Allow that to happen.

These phenomena are called "hypnagogic images," after the Greek god Hypnos who brings hypnosis and sleep. These images appear at the threshold between waking and sleeping, when all of your habitual processes are reversed (you are lying down, not standing; your eyes are closed, not open; your muscles are relaxed, not working). You are too relaxed to want to manipulate your images, and thus this hidden inner world—the reverse of the outer world—comes out to play.

THE INNER WORLD IS ALWAYS THERE

Dusk and dawn, dozing and waking, these induce the twilight states where shapes play tricks on us, where our two worlds meet, mingle, and are sometimes confused with one another. For instance, on waking you have a vivid recall that you put your keys in your handbag. Later on in the day you look for your keys, only to realize that you hadn't *actually* put your keys in your handbag but only dreamt that you had.

Or, as you fall asleep, you are telling your partner to pick your child up from school, but the next day you find out, to your dismay, that you were dreaming when you thought you were talking out loud.

These confusions are completely normal and needn't worry you. Soon you will learn to remain conscious in both worlds at the same time, and these confusions will disappear. In sleep, of course, the inner world appears in dreams (at least you think it does), but so far you are not aware of being conscious of your dreaming while it is actually taking place. You only have memories of it upon waking up. This, too, will change.

The inner world, unlike a vampire, does not disappear at the cock's crow. Imagine the moon is the inner world, the sun the outer world. The moon continues to exist even though it has disappeared from sight. It does not cease to affect the oceans and our bodily fluids while the sun illuminates this side of the planet.

We can say that on one side of the mirror it is always night, on the other side it is always day. Our body is the interface (receiver, transmitter), our perceptual screen, the mirror for both worlds. Since both worlds exist simultaneously, can we not see them equally at the same time and make them one? By the time you finish reading this book you should be able to do just that. Meanwhile, start by asking yourself: has a message from the inner world ever reached through to you during daytime consciousness?

In his book, *And Then There Was Light*, Jacques Lusseyran describes receiving such a message. In fact, Lusseyran was blind, so all he actually *ever* "saw" was his inner world. What makes the reading of his book so interesting is that he describes *how he saw*. As head of the only Youth Resistance movement in France during World War II, he was responsible for choosing all of the movement's officers.

Being blind, how did he do this? Many of the obvious cues that tune us in to someone were missing for him, so he consulted his inner mirror in order to make his selections. This inner mirror responded to his urgent inquiries by presenting him with imaginal configurations.

For instance, when considering one possible candidate for the Resistance movement, a man who was Jacques Lusseyran's *only* choice for operating the crucial Northern Resistance cell, Lusseyran "saw" a great black diagonal cutting across his inner field of perception.

You don't need to be blind to see as he saw. All you need to do is pay attention. I will elaborate on Lusseyran's dilemma in a moment but, in the meantime, see how much of the following exercise you can do.

Daytime Inner Sightings

Close your eyes. Breathe out three times, counting from three to one. Return backward through your life to remember and identify "sightings" similar to Lusseyran's sighting described above. With hindsight, verify whether the information that your sightings conveyed was accurate. Breathe out once and instruct yourself to identify such daytime dream sightings in the future. Breathe out again and open your eyes.

For instance, you are talking to a friend who is telling you a story. You observe his face and hands, but you are also "seeing" him wearing a mask. Later, you learn that everything he told you was a lie. You remember your image. How useful! You have not only "seen," but also have been able *to verify* that what you "saw" was true. At first, only through just such verification will you begin to believe in the messages from your imagination.

Now, returning to the case of Jacques Lusseyran: because there was such urgency to find someone to operate the Northern Resistance cell, he did not allow himself to *trust* his inner eye, which showed him an image of a black diagonal across the man he was considering for the post. Lusseyran ended up choosing this man, with the unfortunate result being that this person later betrayed the whole organization to the Gestapo, and Lusseyran and his friends were sent to Auschwitz.

Inner images are reflecting into the mirror all the time. As you read this you are having them. Either you don't see them or you rarely "see" them, because you have un-learned to accept them as real. But they are there for you to look at and dialogue with when you do decide to focus on them again.

As we have said before, the inner world does not limit itself just to images. Like the outer world, it manifests sounds, words, full sentences, smells, and kinesthetic experiences. But unlike the outer world, these patterns are fluid and volatile. Only by an open, relaxed "watching" can we view them and thus have access to our imagination.

At this point let us pause. Are you ready to admit that imagination is alive and well in you and waiting to play an active role? Are you open to receiving, like the dreamers and seers of the Bible, "messages" from that other "divine" world?

ACCESSING THE INNER WORLD

Imagine that you have been in a dark cave for many days and nights. When you come out into the sunshine the probability is that you will see only swirling colors, hazy shapes, and unfocused scenes which you will misinterpret.

In the same fashion, you have been in the open cave of the outer world far too long, and have forgotten how to "see" in the dark. When you do, the things you see will be fantasies, misinterpretations, and unclear messages. You must learn to "focus" again which means, in the dream world, doing exactly the *reverse* of what is meant by focusing on the outer world.

When you focus in this new world, you scan the whole picture without ever narrowing in on one particular form. You learn to watch a pattern without getting caught *in* the pattern. You teach yourself to focus with increasing concentration until you can "see" the inner world truthfully, unadulterated by a lack of awareness or other disruptions in the field. In other words, you must reeducate yourself.

The language of the inner world is one you knew intimately as a child. You grew up being bilingual, then forgot one of your languages. Because you knew it once, it will be easy for you to learn it again. The trick is to allow yourself to become aware, and then to practice your focus until you recover what William Blake called "true imagination."

When the two worlds—the inner world and the outer world—are equally in focus, they become One. You return to being the first man, whose mirror is a huge, transparent sphere. You become filled with the light illuminating both worlds and *you* become One. This is the ultimate aim of the work that we will undertake in this book.

* * *

To get there you have to accomplish, like the heroes of old, a number of different tasks. You have already accomplished the first task: becoming conscious of the patterns you have been attracted to. Your next task, in preparation for clearing both faces of your mirror, will be to identify all of the disruptions that occur to your mirror which obscure it. How do these disruptions run your life to such an extent that the possibility of change is compromised?

A QUICK REFERENCE GUIDE TO CHAPTER 1 EXERCISES

Identifying Your Strange Attractors: Learn to Recognize What You Are Naturally Drawn To (p. 19)

Take three days to identify and write down, in one column, a list of all of your interests. Then sit down, close your eyes, and breathe out three times. Are there any glaring omissions to your list? See these omissions in images. Give names to the images. Breathe out once. Open your eyes. Write the names of these images down in a separate column.

The Blue Vase: Clear Yourself of Distorted Perceptions (p. 26)

Breathe out all that disturbs you as a light smoke, like a cigarette smoke. Breathe in the radiant blue golden light from the sky, see it filling your nostrils, mouth, and throat, and flowing down your back as a great river of light. See it flowing down into your legs, feet, and toes, and stretching out of your toes as long antennas of light. See the light flowing up your legs into your pelvis and chest, flowing in and out of your heart until it becomes a glowing blue lamp. See the light flow down your arms, fill your hands and fingers, and stretch out as long antennas of light. As you continue to let the light fill you, see it begin to radiate out of your ankles, knees, hips, shoulders, elbows, and wrists. Now the light begins to radiate out of your skin in all directions, until you look like a crystal vase filled with light and radiating light in all directions. Open your eyes, seeing yourself as a crystal vase radiating light in all directions. Hold the image for a few seconds, with open eyes.

The Pendulum: Clear Yourself of Distorted Perceptions (p. 27)

Breathe out three times. Imagine a great crystal pendulum swinging from left to right and back again. Each time the pendulum swings to the right it gathers, into a pile, the disruptions in your life which have caused a narrowing of your choices. Identify each one. Breathe out once. See the pendulum swing wide to the right and, swinging back to the left, in a great sweep, transport the whole pile to the left. Breathe out once. See the pendulum once again swing wide to the right and, swinging back to the left, knock the whole pile off to the left and out of the picture.

Recognizing Daydreams and Fantasies (p. 30)

Spend the next week paying attention to the content of your daydreaming and of your fantasies. Observe them without judgment.

Seeing Hypnagogic Images: Start Your Exploration of Imagination (p. 31)

As you are falling asleep, remain alert and in a restful, suspended, "empty,"watchful state. Watch the flashing colors, the strange disconnected images, or the whole scenes that appear, in vivid detail.

Daytime Inner Sightings (p. 33)

Breathe out three times. Return through your life to remember and identify instances of true vision. With hindsight, verify that the information they conveyed was accurate. Breathe out once. Tell yourself to identify such daytime dream sightings in the future. Breathe out once. Open your eyes.

TWO

The STOP! Game –
Setting Up Your Life Plan

"Rabbi Hiyya said: When the evil inclination (the unexamined impulse) starts to attach itself to a man it is like someone coming to the door (of a house). When he sees that no one tries to stop him, he enters the house and becomes a guest. He notices that no one tries to stop him or send him on his way. Once he has entered the house, and still no one tries to stop him, he gains the upper hand and becomes the master of the house, so that in time he exercises control over the whole household."

ZOHAR II, 267B–268A

"What has been done in time must be undone with time," Colette told me. So many things had been done to me, or so I thought, in the twenty-nine short years before I met Colette that I couldn't bear to think how long it would take to undo the damage. I was depressed, angry, chaotic, emotional, dramatic, needy, teary but, most of all, I was impatient!

I wanted to be all better and cured in a fraction of a second and I wanted Colette to wave her magic wand and do it for me! But that only happens to good girls who, like Cinderella, are not angry or resentful, and who patiently go about their tasks each day without complaining.

I was full of the arrogance and impatience that animates Cinderella's two stepsisters. Like them, I was of two parts; by that I mean I was split, as I seesawed from need to desire back to need again, never satisfied, while my "Inner Cinderella" remained hidden under the cinders of my reactions.

Imagine that you have a spiritual teacher and you are sitting at their feet. This is your first encounter so you are very surprised when a mound of wool gets dropped into your lap. "Untangle this, but don't break any threads, please!" Your teacher never looks at you but you know you are being watched.

Imagine trying to unravel the mess. What do you feel as you face this task? Are you eager to unravel it, or do you feel exhausted just looking at it? As you begin the tedious effort required to unknot the jumble, do you feel an urge to yank it apart? Are you itching to rip the thread? Pay attention to the sensations of your body. We will return to them in a moment.

THE STOP! GAME

In the good old days when extended families lived close together, there were often fifteen kids and just as many grown-ups around the Sabbath table. One of the games that was played at mealtime in Colette's extended family was a game called "STOP!" in which the element of surprise was very important.

No one knew when it would happen during the course of game play, but suddenly one of the grown-ups would call "STOP!" Everyone had to freeze, adults included, even if they were holding a fork midway between their plate and their mouth, or were about to deliver the punch line to a good joke.

Possibly one of the Jews' greatest contributions to the world is the custom of keeping the Sabbath. This is their most holy day, their day of rest. What do they rest *from*? On the Sabbath, religious Jews all over the world play the game of STOP! They stop cooking, they stop lighting matches, they stop switching on the lights. They don't spend money, or write, or cut anything. They don't travel.

To most of us this seems ludicrous, arbitrary, or, at the very least, constraining. There is no TV, there are no movies, no trips to the country or to the mall, no rides in an elevator, no answering the phone. All the fun goes out of life, and this at the end of a week's hard work? What are the Jews doing—are they trying to punish themselves? If so, they've been doing it for centuries without ill effects. And if you ask them, they'll tell you they can't *wait* for the Sabbath to come!

BEAR CUB BOOKS

INNER
TRADITIONS

BEAR & CO.

Inner Traditions • Bear & Company

P.O. Box 388

Rochester, VT 05767-0388

U.S.A.

PLEASE SEND US THIS CARD TO RECEIVE OUR LATEST CATALOG.

Book in which this card was found

_____

❑ Check here if you would like to receive our catalog via e-mail.

Name_____ Company_____

Address_____ Phone_____

City_____ State_____ Zip_____ Country_____

E-mail address_____

Please check the following area(s) of interest to you:

❑ Health   ❑ Self-help   ❑ Science/Nature   ❑ Shamanism

❑ Ancient Mysteries   ❑ New Age/Spirituality   ❑ Ethnobotany   ❑ Martial Arts

❑ Spanish Language   ❑ Sexuality/Tantra   ❑ Children   ❑ Teen

Please send a catalog to my friend:

Name_____ Company_____

Address_____ Phone_____

City_____ State_____ Zip_____ Country_____

Order at 1-800-246-8648 • Fax (802) 767-3726

E-mail: customerservice@InnerTraditions.com • Web site: www.InnerTraditions.com

THE MYSTERY OF STOP!

Let's look at this mystery more closely. All the activities I've mentioned above are things we do every day. We don't think about switching on a light. We just do it. It is natural to use a pen to write, natural to pick up the phone when it rings, or to put your hand into your purse for money. We perform these gestures each day of our lives without questioning them.

Yet every seventh day, orthodox Jews refrain from carrying out these everyday gestures. Find one thing you are addicted to, such as flipping on the TV when you wake up and/or when you come home from work. Choose a day wherein you decide you are not going to watch TV at all. Try it. Soon you'll find yourself engaged in a tug-of-war between your will and your need; all you can think about is TV!

Your mind will be constructing all sorts of excuses why it is silly to give up watching TV and why there is no reason in the world that you cannot watch it. The more you think about it, the harder it gets. The TV starts talking at you in the same way that Richard Pryor, in one of his comedy routines, described his cocaine pipe talking to him: "What you go'na do, Rich? What you go'na do?"

That's when most of us give in and, with a sigh of relief, revert to our old habits. But this doesn't happen without a backlash. The need reacts like a voracious dog that, having been given a piece of the kill, wants the whole carcass. Wouldn't it be great to be able to stop? To say "no" to the TV, the cigarette, the food, the kinky sex, or whatever pattern you've noticed has taken over? To say "no" and, in so doing, be the master of your needs rather than their slave?

BUILDING A CORRAL

Imagine your needs as a wild horse. You are engaged in a tug-of-war, trying to subdue the horse. If all you have are your lasso and your strength, you will soon tire out. The horse's superior strength will certainly get the better of you.

But imagine that you have come to the contest prepared—you have built a corral for the horse! Step by step you back up until you have pulled the horse into the corral where you can close the gate behind it. The corral is the third element in the equation. As such, it breaks open the closed polarity of the tug-of-war between your will and your needs and makes it possible for something new to happen.

Habits are ingrained in the body. You must work with the body if you wish to change your habits. The Jews, understanding this well, did something very clever. They built the corral by teaching the body the habit of saying "no" on every seventh day (their version of the STOP! game). There is a rhythm in seven that the body understands (our cells reproduce every seventh day, for example).

Remember Doctor Pavlov's famous dogs? When the bell rang, they were given food. So they became habituated to wanting food when the bell rang. In the same way for the Jews keeping the Sabbath, when the seventh day comes, the body wants to say "no" because it has learned the habit, and the habit is sweet to it.

THE AIM OF THE GAME

Just gaining some control over our needs is rewarding in itself. But there is more to it than that. The Jews clearly spelled out their intention when they wrote down the laws for keeping the Sabbath. "Don't switch on a light, don't answer the phone, etc." They wanted to bring down the extra soul of the Sabbath, which they call *Shechina*, "the Divine Feminine." Kabbalists were known to go out in the field to greet the bride, the Shechina, at the onset of the Sabbath.

To understand this concept, let's go back to the horse for a moment. The horse's strength is phenomenal, but of no use to man if the horse is wild. By bringing the horse into the corral and training it, man harnesses the horse's strength and gains its power for his own needs. In the same way the Jews, by reigning in *their* instinctual nature, make this great energy available for positive, creative purposes. They bring into themselves extra soul, vital energy.

However, this cannot be done without a longing for something other than what you have. You cannot simply eliminate a habit and then sit back and expect that you have mastered your need. *To be successful, you must replace this old habit with another "better" habit.*

Imagine that, like the two stepsisters in the Cinderella story, you are very impatient. This impatience is your horse, wild and unpredictable. So much power exists in the energy of your impatience, but it's of no use to you because you have not harnessed it. Worse, it has gone rampant and is creating havoc in your life.

What would you do with this power if you could harness it? Stay a moment now with that question.

Identifying One of Your Goals

Draw a circle and, when you get an answer to the question above, write it down in the circle. You have just targeted a goal, you have created your intent.

We will be discussing this later in chapter 8, but before we get there we have much other work to do.

* * *

THE BEAUTY OF INSTINCTS

What has all this got to do with the second task of the dreamer and the subject of this chapter: identifying what obscures the mirror? Do our uncontrolled instincts cloud the mirror of truth? Are they so bad that we need to stop them? Remember the mass of tangled wool at the beginning of this chapter? It is still in your hands where your teacher put it, waiting to be unraveled. But your instincts are calling you outside. You want to gambol in the field, not unravel wool!

Is this bad? Your instincts are young, wild, untamed. It is their nature to be so, as it is the horse's nature to frisk, buck, and gallop. What could be more beautiful than nature unshackled, free, playful, and powerful? A wild stallion prancing on a hill? A majestic ocean wave, a raging torrent?

Introduce a baby into a group of adults apparently engrossed in talking to one another and you'll soon see every one of them shift their attention to the baby. Baby breathes, gesticulates, smiles, gurgles, baby's naturalness enchants us—even more, it enthralls us. We, too, want to revert back to nature, we smile and gurgle with baby. We long to possess this innocence.

But, as my five-year-old friend Kay, who was jealous of her baby sister, soon found out when she insisted on trying it, returning to diapers and suckling isn't fun. Pretending innocence is silly. Nor, of course, does it in any way clear the mirror to give us a truthful picture of the world. In Kay's case, baby sister will still be getting most of Mom's attention, and Kay's jealousy will remain unassuaged.

Whether she likes it or not, Kay's instincts have misled her into trying to be only one year old, when she actually is five. It is not her instincts that are bad or cloud the mirror, but what has *happened* to them on the way to their attempted fulfillment. How did Kay lose her innocence, her enchanted garden where she had Mom all to herself? How did her mirror become clouded?

LIFE IS MOVEMENT

Our span of life can be compared to a clock with a certain wind-up time. There are yogis who teach that we are programmed from birth to breathe a specific number of breaths. These yogis say the number of breaths we are programmed to take in our lifetime varies from person to person, depending on our karma and destiny. For our purposes let's call this wind-up time our "basic vital energy." This is the energy we have at our disposal which, as the yogis have pointed out, differs markedly from person to person, some of us being born with abundant energy, some not. As we shall see, though, the issue is not so much how abundant our energy supply is but how we *manage* the energy that we do have.

You can imagine your vital energy as a tightly wound coil. Before birth this primal energy lies largely dormant. At birth, maybe the most dramatic moment of our life, when air rushes in to fill our empty lungs, (or should we say, is sucked in by the vacuum of our empty lungs) and—like our wild horse who bucks at being touched, our lungs, force-filled, kick out the air—the coil is released, setting us in motion.

Spirit has been released and we are alive, a new being taking its place in the outer world. Strange attractors—empty lungs and air—have found each other. From the initial shock of their meeting, the whole pathway and form of their interaction is forged into a pattern of exhaling and inhaling.

The impulse of the empty lungs to kick back when incited or pricked by the air is what we call an "instinctual reflex" (from the Latin *instinguere*, "to incite," and *stinguere*, "to prick"). We can say that our *instinct* is to breathe out.

In the same way, the first encounter of eyes and light stimulates the impulse to see forms; the first sounds activating our ear drums stimulate the impulse to hear sounds; the first meeting of body and space stimulates the impulse to move; skin and touch stimulate the impulse for contact; an empty stomach stimulates the impulse to eat; too much stimuli stimulates the impulse to shut down and sleep.

Did anyone tell you to do these things? No! Breathing, seeing, hearing, moving, searching for contact, boundaries, food, sleep, are all reflexes and instincts, impulsive movements in response to outside stimuli. Our inner nature encounters outside nature and habits of interaction are formed.

After their initial interaction, these movements, like the pendulum of a clock, will swing back and forth without your having to make them happen. Once your vital energy is set in motion, it has to keep on moving.

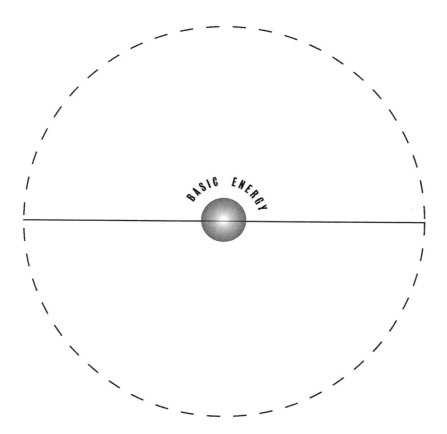

Figure 1. Basic Energy. Before birth our basic vital energy lies dormant.

HOW INSTINCTS GET DEFLECTED

Can our instincts be simply blocked? Can a raging torrent wait? If it is arrested by a boulder which has slid down the mountainside to land exactly in its pathway, will the torrent just stop running and wait for the rock to move away?

Of course not! It builds up until it overflows the barrier. Your instincts are like the raging torrent—they have to go *somewhere*. Imagine that you can't breathe. If this goes on for just a short time, you'll die. As the instinctual movement is floundering—your arms are flailing, your heart beats crazily—you are in a panic. The movement has shifted from its natural groove (breathing) to become something other: an emotion.

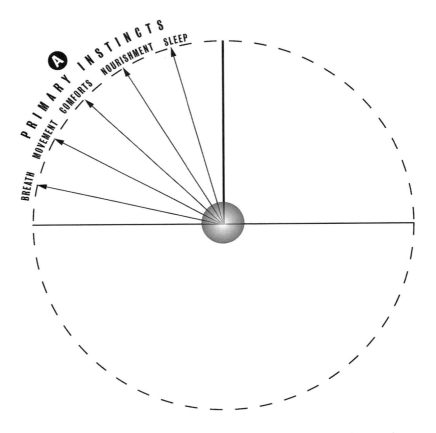

Figure 2. Primary Instincts. Our basic energy is triggered by our first encounter with the outside world. At birth the pathways of relationship with the outer world are established. The baby breathes, moves, searches for warmth and touch, for food and for rest.

Note how "e-motion" contains the word "motion" and the prefix "e" which is Latin for "coming from." Blocking an instinctual movement is like blocking the raging torrent. Tension builds and builds, to the point where something has to give. If you were the wild horse that is being dragged to the corral, wouldn't your breathing stop in shock? Wouldn't you buck and kick to shake the rope loose? And when that doesn't work, wouldn't you attack?

What of little Kay, when her plan for getting rid of her little sister by imitating and replacing her is thwarted? She too is capable of bucking and kicking to get attention, or she may even resort to attacking her little sister.

Our primary "e-motions" are fear and anger. They are signaled by a change in breathing patterns, and in heartbeats which quicken and become erratic, in chaotic movements, or in "re-actions" such as cowering or lashing out. (See figure 3.)

WHEN THE MIRROR GETS MUDDIED

Does fear cloud the mirror? Is fear bad? If we had no fear, our survival would soon be threatened. When survival is at stake the animal in us runs or attacks. Are these reactions wrong? At this *primary level* emotion is very useful, and therefore good.

Imagine that you are a prehistoric hunter who has just killed an antelope. Suddenly you hear a growl and turning, find yourself face-to-face with a tiger who wants your antelope. What do you feel and do? This primeval man is scared and enraged.

In the same way, when our breathing is jeopardized, our movements constrained, our food supply taken away, our sleep interrupted, or when we are deprived of warmth and touch, we react in a very primal way. We express our fear and anger by running from, or attacking, the one who threatens us. When this instinctual reaction is allowed to reach its goal unimpeded, when we are allowed to express our fear or rage fully, the mirror is not clouded.

Unfortunately, as little Kay found out, we do not live in the wild. Her anger might be a healthy *primitive* reaction, but expressing it by attacking her little sister is not acceptable. Not only does she not get her mom back, but her mom is displeased and Kay gets sent to her room! Now that is really unfair, she is only doing what is *natural!* What is she going to do with her fear and her anger? Remember—the movement must go somewhere, for once it is triggered it cannot stop moving until, like a wave, it has exhausted its potential.

While Kay is smoldering in her room she tries telling herself a story: Once upon a time there was a terrible dragon who lived in a cave and preyed upon the countryside. He sallied forth to kill little sisters.

In her anger Kay very much wants this story to be true, but alas, it is only a fantasy of her own invention! And fantasies, as we have established in chapter 1, disrupt the pure reflection of our inner world by feeding our needy, thwarted expectations.

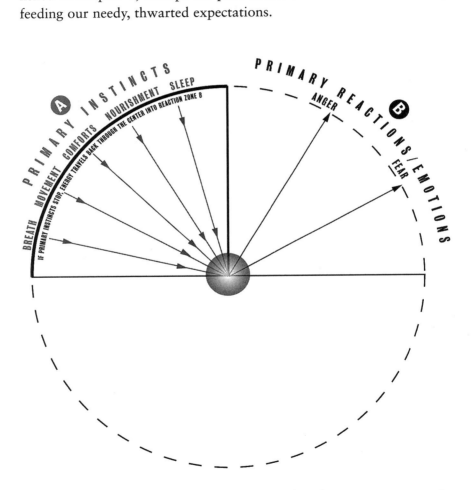

Figure 3. Primary Reactions/Emotions. When, for whatever reason, one of our instinctual movements is blocked, the energy must travel somewhere: it becomes a primary reaction/emotion of fear or anger.

In her room, Kay paces back and forth like a wild beast in a cage, finally crouching in a corner to wallow in self-pity and resentment. The pure arc of her anger at the outside world is interrupted and catapulted back into her small body. Caught there, it shows up in dissipated body movements or goes very still, like stagnant water, either outcome muddying her clear inner mirror.

Frustration, resentment, guilt, irritation, anxiety, envy, depression, sadness—have I named them all? (See figure 4.) These are what we call "secondary reactions." They represent caught energies that often

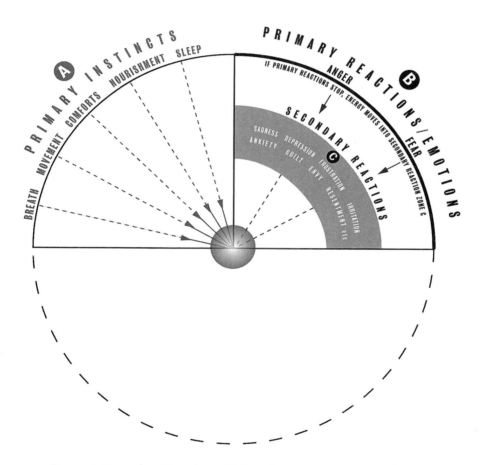

Figure 4. Secondary Reactions. If, for whatever reason, our primary reactions/emotions of anger or fear are blocked and we cannot express them, the energy must move somewhere else. It travels to Secondary Reactions, a stagnant pool of trapped movement.

seesaw from the emotional realm back to the instinctual realm. In this way we develop habits which masquerade as instincts.

For example, frustration may seesaw back to smoking, or sadness may seesaw back to overeating, loveless sex, excessive sleeping, or even illness. These unresolved emotional knots lie at the origin of our irresistible needs and addictions, such as drug taking, alcoholism, or uncontrollable masturbation. We call these irresistible needs and addictions "secondary instincts." (See figure 5.)

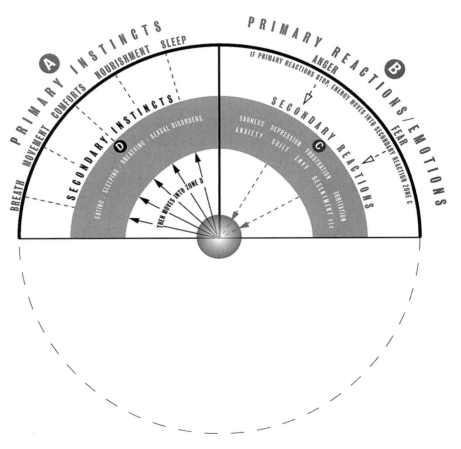

Figure 5. Secondary Instincts. From the pool of stagnant secondary emotions, some energy inevitably leaks back to false instinctual behaviors. All eating, sleeping, breathing, sexual disorders, agitations/paralysis, addictions, etc. . . . fit in here.

SIN AND REPRESSION

If you throw a heavy stone into clear waters, sands will rise and turn the waters muddy. As a result, you won't be able to see the beautiful rocks and colorful fish that live there. Secondary emotions act like that, they obscure our vision of the mirror.

Does this mean we shouldn't be emotional? The Christian Church says that impatience, greed, sadness, and the plethora of other emotions mentioned earlier are sins. If you don't sin, you'll go to Heaven, if you persist in your bad ways you'll go to Hell.

But it is all too easy to say that we should stop being impatient, sad, or frustrated. It is much harder to know *how* to stop. Should we repress our emotions? As we have seen, repression is exactly where the problem lies. If Kay doesn't express her anger, it reverts or collapses inward.

Have you ever looked at a wave as it hits a seawall? The wave will splash and foam against the barrier, and then eddy backward to whence it came. We are all "sinners" in the eyes of the Church. Should we accept the finger pointed at us, should we just give up and believe that we are *bad*? Or instead, should we think more carefully about the forces directing the flow of our emotions?

Is Kay *bad*? Are Cinderella's two stepsisters bad? In terms of their social behavior they are but, in terms of the truth, it is more accurate to say that they are *misdirected. The truth is that there is no sin, only a lack of awareness of where to direct the great waves of our emotions.* Heaven and Hell are right here now for us. The muddy waters are our Hell because they obscure the clear waters and the rocks and colorful fish that are Heaven for us to watch.

If you throw more rocks into the water—for instance, you say to yourself that you are bad because you can't stop feeling resentful and self-pitying—then you are adding the stone called "guilt" to the stones already collecting at the bottom of the water. If you do this often enough, the waters may become chronically muddy.

You sense, like the two bad stepsisters, that Heaven exists, since you too dream about marrying the Prince. But the Prince cannot see you, because you are not wearing Cinderella's glass slippers.

LEARNING TO OBSERVE OUR REACTIONS

If the Prince cannot see you, you probably can't see yourself either. You know that something isn't quite right, but you can't pinpoint what it is because the waters are too muddied by now for you to make any sense of where you're at. You feel you're in a bad dream, and as tangled up as the knotted mass of wool you are still holding in your hands.

How can you step back and take a look? Simple: Watch your *reactions* to the knotted wool. What do they tell you? Remember, they are neither good nor bad. At this point, you are not judging, simply looking. Does the wool make you feel mad, frustrated, sad, or excited? Pay attention to your body, for it is in the body that these emotions manifest; the body has the keys to what you are looking for.

Secondary Instincts/Secondary Emotions List

Let's agree that you get a little notebook, small enough to put in your shirt pocket or in your bag. Make two columns, one for "secondary instincts" on the left, the other for "secondary emotions" on the right. Every day for a week record your secondary emotions and instincts. Mark them down in the order in which they appear. For instance, you woke up feeling irritated: mark that down in the column on the right. You smoked a cigarette just after that, although you had decided never to smoke before noon: mark that down in the column on the left. Continue to record your secondary emotions and instincts in the order in which they appear throughout the day. Do this for a week, without judging yourself. Just record what is happening. By the end of the week you should have a fair sample of the way you react and how you compensate by reverting back to secondary instincts. You will be able to see exactly how your energy swings back and forth. You might find that you are writing the same thing over and over again, for instance, "smoking . . . frustration." Don't feel bad, and don't try to change anything just yet.

You are learning to *observe*. Being able to observe yourself is the first step in clearing the mirror, while recording your movements brings your observations into concrete focus.

THE LIFE PLAN

Now that you can clearly see yourself stepping into the same pothole over and over again, like the hero in the movie *Groundhog Day*, aren't you beginning to ask yourself some very basic questions? You don't want to become that bitter old woman or that resentful old man you are setting yourself up to be. You have just spread out the map and identified your obstacles. You know which perilous roads and congested towns to avoid; they look like your worst nightmares or recurring dreams. And while you haven't yet identified what it is you *do* want, at least now you are on the right road to finding that out. You are just beginning to set up your "Life Plan" (refer back to figures 1 through 5).

While the idea of a Life Plan may sound somewhat grandiose, it is in fact a very simple concept. We all have a Life Plan, even if, for some of us, the picture of our Life Plan is somewhat nebulous. But not to worry: guiding you to envision your Life Plan and then to bring it to manifestation is the aim of this book! The journey will take you through the forest of your imagination where you will encounter the wild beasts of your emotions, your secondary emotions, and your secondary instincts, all of which are costumed and masked like Halloween tricksters.

You will learn how to engage these protagonists of your imagination. As you confront them, play with them, tame them, and transform them, you will be teaching yourself how not to react. In so doing, learning to catch your reactions at the very instant of their inception will help to clarify your dreaming. Along the way, you will get clearer and clearer about who you truly are—and who you want to become. There are a number of maneuvers you must commit to before you can hope to perfect your Life Plan.

MASTER OF THE STOP! GAME

Meanwhile, life plays the STOP! game with us all the time. The horse is captured, Kay's little sister is born, the boulder falls in the pathway of the torrent. Life is movement and change and there is nothing we can do about that. Or is there? Wouldn't it be better if, instead of being the victims of life's vagaries, we could become the master of the STOP! game and catch our emotions as they arise in order to transmute them?

But this requires much clarity and foresight. Remember, the aim of the game is to redirect your energy and you have only *just* begun to untangle the mass of knotted wool. There is a long way to go before you can untangle all of the threads of your life and play the master game of Stop! But, like Cinderella's two stepsisters, I'm sure you can visualize the Prince of your dreams and, like them, you can conjure up your "Inner Cinderella." Her qualities are those you most aspire to have.

Life Plan List of Qualities

Make a list of those qualities that you most aspire to have, as they come up for you, on a separate page in your little notebook.

In this way you will be setting your goal, or "intent" as we have called it. For kabbalists, their intent is clearly the Shechina. For you, it would be those qualities that you have just identified. Thus, you start the process of clarifying for yourself what your Life Plan truly is.

* * *

You have begun to tease out and to identify the disruptions that cloud your mirror and obscure the pure message of your imagination. This will make it easier for you to face the third task of the dreamer: confronting the muddied dreams, the products of those disruptions acting on your imagination, that you have not wanted or been able to look at.

A QUICK REFERENCE GUIDE TO CHAPTER 2 EXERCISES

Identify One of Your Goals (p. 41)

Breathe out three times. See a circle. Within the circle see, appearing in gold letters, your most pressing goal. Breathe out once. Open your eyes. See your goal with open eyes; this is your "intent."

Secondary Instincts/Secondary Emotions List (p. 50)

List, in two separate columns, your secondary instincts and secondary emotions. Take a week to mark them down as they appear.

Life Plan List of Qualities (p. 52)

Make a list of those qualities that you most aspire to have, as they come up for you, on a separate page in your little notebook.

THREE

Paying Attention to Your Dreams

"A dream that is not interpreted is like a letter that is not read. And come and see. If one does not remember it, it is as if one had never known it. Therefore whoever forgets a dream and does not know it, will not benefit from its fulfillment."

ZOHAR I, 199B–200A

Like any self-respecting hero from the world of myth, we must be willing to fight our dragons, traverse our swamps, and cut through the tangled briars of our emotions. We can't expect to awaken our "Inner Cinderella" or win our Prince without facing dangers and passing trials of strength.

But few of us are equipped from birth, as the Greek hero Hercules was, to strangle magic serpents sent to kill us in our cradle (childhood trauma), then go on to conquer our Nemean lion (anger) and clean out our infested Augean stables (stagnation of secondary emotions: guilt, resentment, frustration, irritation, depression, sadness, despair, discouragement, indolence, laziness, cowardice, etc.).

Instead of acting like heroes, we tend to hold back, afraid of unleashing our murderous rages onto the world. Once securely established in a state of repression, we steel ourselves for a long siege and, armed to the teeth, set up defense mechanisms to repulse the imaginary enemy outside of ourselves. Or, in imitation of a panic-stricken ostrich, we bury our heads in the sand, hoping the storm will pass. But the storm is *in* us, trapping us in a negative spin, and it will not abate unless we face it and do something about it.

Of course, we cannot stop ourselves from feeling the storm of negative secondary emotion inside us. How could we *not* feel it, when it thrashes about in our bodies with such force? We cramp, we tense, we contort; the sensations are often so painful we recoil from them. It is possible we could begin to deal with the storm if we allowed ourselves to focus on our sensations.

But instead of working on our pain's real source we project it outward and blame the world, the people around us. Or we isolate the pain, thinking we can starve it to death by ignoring it.

We can use the story of another ancient Greek hero to illustrate our plight. Prometheus stole fire from the gods to bring life and enlightenment to humankind. For this act, Zeus punished him by chaining him to a barren cliff where an eagle came every morning to tear out his liver, which then regenerated every night to make his torture unending. If we allow ourselves to feel our defensive, immobilized state we can see how much we resemble Prometheus.

Like him, we are seeking light but we are chained to a rock (the stagnation of secondary emotions), while our pent-up rage, turned inward, attacks us in the guise of an eagle devouring our insides. The fire we had hoped to bring to the world burns instead in our intestines. Do we have the courage to contemplate such a nightmare?

IGNORING THE EMOTIONS BEHIND NIGHTMARES

"An eagle is eating my tummy!" cries Julian.

"Don't be silly, it's only a dream," says his mother, lighting the bedside lamp. "See, there's nothing here!" (meaning out here in the tangible world). She ignores or forgets that what's important is that there is something *inside* of Julian.

"I don't want to tell you about my dream, it's too frightening," says Cynthia to her father.

His reply, "So forget it, go back to sleep!" doesn't alter the fact that Cynthia has a hard time going back to sleep; the intruder is still pursuing her when she closes her eyes. Nightmares don't vanish so easily. How can they, since they are our perception of chaotic sensations produced by our very *real* emotions?

Chances are, if nothing is done to help Julian and Cynthia, they'll continue to be haunted by nightmares for years to come. As adults, they'll take sleeping pills to avoid facing the call from their subconscious and, when their level of drug tolerance has been reached, they'll drug themselves some more.

But are they to blame? They run away from themselves because they are desperate and don't know any better; they haven't been given the tools to deal with the frightening images within.

BACKED-UP ENERGY AS "DIS-EASE"

Fortunately, in most cases, it is not possible to run away forever. The backed-up energy will eventually erupt, forcing us to pay attention and to seek help. Remember that once set in motion, thwarted instincts and emotions must go somewhere. If they can't get our attention through violent dreams, they will get it in other ways. The build-up leaks out where there is a crack in the armor and, once out, takes on a form suited to the level of our being where it appears, flaunting itself as a "dis-ease" in an otherwise easeful body.

Disease can manifest at four different levels: the physical (diarrhea, heart palpitations, facial tics, postural changes, etc.); the emotional (fantasies, illusions, destructive patterns of behavior, etc.); the mental (obsessions, compulsions, schizothymia, paranoia, etc.); and the spiritual (indolence, indifference, bitterness, accidie, loss of meaning, apostasy, etc.).

One thing you may be sure of, if there is backed-up energy, disease will eventually make its appearance at one of those levels of your being. Can you imagine living in a house where a supporting wall is cracked? If you can't trust the stability of your own home, you won't find much enjoyment in your life. Your anxiety and obsession about the cracked wall can cause you to lose your healthy grip on reality. Added to this, instead of dealing with the *source* of your disease, you are now obsessing about its effects.

But how can we get at the source, if we can't or won't allow ourselves to "see"? Can the effects or symptoms alone offer a way to enlighten us? What do they have in common?

BELL-LIKE SYMPTOMS

Remember our timid ostrich at the beginning of this chapter? In its anxiety it has now swallowed some leftover lunch, a paper bag, a cigarette butt, string, keys, and finally an old alarm clock. All these objects are milling around in its stomach, and soon the ostrich has indigestion. But instead of doing something about it, it unhappily sticks its head in the sand, its rump and feathers hanging out.

Suddenly, the alarm clock in the ostrich's stomach, set off by all the agitation, begins to ring repetitively every thirty seconds. *If I don't move,* thinks the ostrich, *no one will hear the alarm!* Who is the ostrich trying to fool? Of course we hear, and it hears, the bell-like sound—the symptom—waving at us; the call repeated over and over to wake up, pay attention, and do something more enterprising, more adventurous than just sticking our heads in the sand!

How many times have you come across people who can't stop rehashing their past, who talk incessantly about their failed love affair, the boss who humiliated them, or the friend who stole their money? What about people who obsess about their appearance or about their physical pains? How about people who repeat the same mistakes over and over, as if they can never learn?

Then there are those people who tell the same old jokes, or the same old war stories, or use a word over and over, like "great . . . great . . . great" every time you say something, or who nod their heads to punctuate each one of your sentences? Do you remember how this makes you feel? How you become unfocused, disconnected, sleepy, and desperate to get away from them? This is unfortunate because it is exactly the opposite effect these people want to make.

Nobody heard him, the dead man,
But still he lay moaning:
I was much further out than you thought
And not waving but drowning.
Poor chap, he always loved larking
And now he's dead
It must have been too cold for him his heart gave way,
They said.
Oh, no no no, it was too cold always

(Still the dead one lay moaning)
I was much too far out all my life
And not waving but drowning.

"Not Waving But Drowning," Stevie Smith,
The Collected Poems of Stevie Smith, 1957

We reason that it's better to ignore the dead man's waving than drown with him. After all, if his vital energy is trapped, why should ours be? We've seen how repetitiveness has a lulling, even hypnotic, effect on us. Worse, we've seen how we begin to mirror the other person's stuckness.

We feel like the fly caught in a spider's web of conflicting emotions. *We* also tend to rehash; in this case the thought that keeps coming back is that we ought to listen to our friend, since the man is obviously suffering. Yet all we really want to do is run away, but we don't because we don't want to hurt his feelings. In our minds we dismiss him as an old, doting bore. Meanwhile, the alarm bell of his repetitive behavior continues to ring every thirty seconds.

We have listened only to the *drone,* we haven't heard the force of *emotional meaning* behind the repetitive alarm bell! Just as when we hear a car alarm sounding in the street, we try to turn it off in our minds, hoping it will soon stop. But we don't do the obvious—thereby fulfilling the reason for which the car alarm was designed in the first place—we don't go check to see if someone is actually breaking into the car.

The alarm bell is screeching, "Wake up, pay attention!" Likewise, your friend is waving to attract your attention: "Help, help, I'm drowning in a storm of my own making and I can't save myself without your help!"

Repetitiveness is a call for help. It is its own best advertiser and worst enemy; it works like a trapped bat bumping into walls. The bumps are saying, "Get me out of here!" but in the dark, their very repetitiveness might put us to sleep!

RECOGNIZING BELL-LIKE
SYMPTOMS IN OURSELVES

So far we have only talked of other people's bell-like symptoms. What about yours? Can you identify them? Now that you have a technique to help yourself, it shouldn't be too hard. Look for your own repetitive behavior. Do not be afraid to own up to it. We are all caught in some form of repetitive behavior, simply because we are human. It is the nature of our world to be limited by form and habit. Soon you will see the transformative advantage of tracking down such behavior and consciously examining it.

Check yourself. Do you have a bell-word, like "awesome," "whatever," or "sharing"? Do you have tics, like twirling your hair or cracking your knuckles? Do you have set patterns of behavior, like eating when you're worried, or calling your boyfriend late at night to check up on him? Do you always get into the same type of destructive relationships, always have trouble at work or with money? Do you regularly indulge in the same type of fantasies: romantic, sexual, or violent?

Clara's fantasy is of a castle on a hill, illuminated by a full moon. High up in the castle is the open window of a bedroom lit by soft light, and out of the window leans a handsome young man. Clara looks up longingly. This fantasy, animated by her vague longings for someone important in her life, is replayed *ad nauseum* in her mind, as it is replayed in many a romance novel.

Roger's fantasy is to be the hero who kills many evil monsters and conquers everyone who stands in his way. Usually driven by feelings of anger, this fantasy is nothing new; you've seen endless variations of it on your TV and movie screens.

Identifying Your Repetitive Behavior

Watch yourself for a few days to identify your repetitive patterns of behavior. Pay attention to repetitive postures, gestures, expressions, mimicry; to repetitive words, sentences, jokes, stories; to repetitive patterns of behavior. If you keep watching what you're doing, you're going to get tired of always doing or saying the same thing.

You'll know where to look because repetitiveness always makes you sleepy, unfocused, moody, disconnected, out of it. If you feel these symptoms, start paying attention. Becoming aware of your bell-like symptoms shouldn't cause you to despair. On the contrary, you should rejoice because you have found the tail of one of the beasts you must hunt down!

As a hero, it is all-important for you to find worthy adversaries to fight. Grab onto this tail for all you're worth and pull. Soon the whole beast will appear.

But isn't that exactly what you fear most? Coming face-to-face with the beast of your anger or your fears? You have followed me thus far, far enough to know that running away or hiding is not for you. You must now decide that you have had enough of disease, boredom, and wasted energy. The time has come when you have no better choice than to face your inner demons. Have a heart and, like the hero-in-training that you are, bravely go forth! The tools to conquer will be given to you.

* * *

FEARS OR PATTERNS

All of us, like the great wizard Merlin, are born with the power to "see" beneath surface appearances. Our nightmares—disruptive and violent—also teach us that none of us are completely safe from the dangers that come with having this gift. Instead of fearing and ignoring it, how can we handle such power? How can we learn to "see" in comparative safety? But before that, what does "seeing" really mean?

As we have said in chapter 1, everything depends on pattern and the affinities that lie beneath pattern. Where interaction exists, there is a pattern. Pattern is the manifest form of relationships. For instance, the relationship of a river to its rocky bed may create eddies and vortexes. For the traveler attempting to cross the river, these eddies and vortexes are dangers he fears. That night, the same eddies and vortexes may appear in his dream as vicious serpents that coil around his legs to pull him down to the green depths below.

But for the local boatman who has run the river all his life, these eddies and vortexes do not appear as serpents but as indicators he can use to enable his journey. Because of his experience in observing the eddies, he can read their pattern, which shows him how the current is affected by underwater obstructions and how deep these obstructions might lie.

Imagine you have a nightmare in which an intruder breaks into your house. This is a frightening event, so frightening that you wake up screaming. But now, like the boatman, take another look at this frightening image, for experience has taught you how to read its pattern; you have learned to recognize how important parts of yourself are behind it.

In this case, the image of an intruder is energized by a part of yourself you have held back until it has been forced to use violent methods—the nightmare—to get your attention. By learning to look at the nightmare as a pattern, you "see" it and you start to disengage from the purely frightening elements of its story.

"SEEING" IS MORE THAN LOOKING

Pattern in the imagination is never static. To borrow the words of James Glieck who writes about chaos theory, it is a "shape embedded in the fabric of motion." If pattern does appear to be stagnant or repetitive, it simply means that its energy has gone dormant. Being stuck is a clear sign to us that pattern has to be brought back to life.

I give the name "Merlin" to this ability to make pattern move again in our lives. Merlin is the "seeing" aspect in each of us. There is a story about Merlin which shows this "seeing" aspect at work.

Vortigern, King of the Britons, wanted to build a mighty tower to protect his people from invading pagans, but no sooner is the tower built than it collapses. Over and over, like a recurring nightmare, it crumbles to the ground. Like our dreaming traveler who faced surging waters, King Vortigern is filled with fear.

Consumed by his fear, he has no chance of "seeing" why the tower is forever collapsing. Eventually he gives up trying to force the tower to stand and goes in search of help. Clearly, "seeing" requires something more than just looking. King Vortigern calls for Merlin, the young boy who, people say, has no father (no causal origin) and can "see" things.

Merlin, when he arrives, settles himself on a little hilltop, removed from the scene. This detail of the story confirms what we stated above, that "seeing" requires distance, detachment, and looking at the overall picture from afar. In this story, Merlin is depicted as a young boy with a pure, clear gaze. "Seeing" also requires looking with the eyes of a young child, who happens to be both pragmatic and imaginative in equal measure.

If a young child's toy tower collapses, the child will inspect it from above, from the sides, from below. He checks that the sky is clear and that what he can see of the earth looks solid. This leaves the part of the earth that he *can't* see—the underground—as the only possible source of disruption. How does he look underground? Here is an exercise to show you how to try it yourself.

Looking below the Surface

Locate in your life an area of repetitive failure. Instead of being enslaved to your failure by forever looking outward, as King Vortigern does with his collapsing tower, allow your eyes to turn inward and to journey down to the source of the failure. What is the first image you see? Breathe out and open your eyes.

This mythic story is giving you permission to "see." By entering it to tap your source, you uncover a new and possibly more effective way of dealing with an old personal problem, in this case, the pain you experience from chronic failure.

What Merlin "saw" when he shifted his gaze, i.e., changed his vantage point to look below the chronic pain of the collapsing tower, was an underground lake. Building a tower over an unstable foundation makes no sense.

Within the lake were two dragons, one red, one white; both fast asleep and locked in a mortal grip. What more graphic image of hidden, conflicting emotions could there be than these two grappling opposites imprisoned in the unstable, earthbound pool of our subconscious? King Vortigern wisely decided to stop building his tower, and instead contemplated the pattern that the tower's collapse was showing him.

"SEEING" IS NOT ANALYZING

The story continues. It describes how, as King Vortigern watches and is truly able to "see," (having learnt to do this from Merlin), the dragons wake up. "Seeing," the story implies, is active, or should I say "interactive." *The relationship of "seeing" to the pattern, has changed the pattern.* Awakened by Merlin's and Vortigern's "seeing," the dragons rise in the sky, what had been suppressed finally comes to pass, and the dragons fight a battle to the death.

Eventually the red dragon falls, leaving the white dragon as victor. The conflicting emotions, brought to the surface and given space to do battle by the act of "seeing," have come to resolution; the best dragon wins. King Vortigern, leaving his tower unfinished, returns home a chastened and more real human being.

Someone once complained to me that "seeing" is too simplistic. In "seeing," no attempt is made to analyze the different motives in the story-in-the-dream. However, as far as we know, the tower is not a symbol of some inner phallic repression or royal ambition; the two dragons and their battle are not your mother and father; the story is not a myth or an allegory.

"Seeing" does not require us to do this work. Let's leave the analyzing, the categorizing, to Freudians and Jungians who do this much better than we do. We do not concern ourselves with symbols. Symbols—objects, drawings, ceremonies—are outer representations of something intangible. Intangible, that is, to all but our Merlin—our "seeing" aspect—which is the sacred within all of us.

The act of "seeing" returns us to the sacred. In life, the sacred demands from us that we respect what our inner senses tell us: "Believe your own eyes." "Seeing" is simple, it is the innocent looking of a child-like consciousness, free from fears and preconceived ideas.

So put away your dream dictionaries, your encyclopedias of symbols, your nomenclatures of archetypes. Just watch the pattern unfold as you dream. It tells you, far better than any explanation originating outside of yourself, what is happening *within* you. Granted, it does this in often fearful, awesome, but surely beautiful ways that speak to you directly about your emotions, your power, and your hidden vitality.

Remember that each part of the pattern—each part of the dream—is a part of yourself. And because myth and legend are also dream, the king, Merlin, the tower, the lake, the dragons—all are also aspects of yourself interacting together. How these different aspects of yourself weave themselves into a grand tapestry for your "seeing" will always be more meaningful, more vital, more real than any theory found in any book. Stay simple and watch what your pattern is showing you.

* * *

TYPES OF PATTERNS YOU ENCOUNTER
AT THIS LEVEL

Dreams are our primary way of "seeing" because they occur at night when we are turned inward; thus they are available to inner perception. This is the time when we are completely relaxed and unguarded, our eyes are closed, our posture supine. Night dreams are our most direct route to "seeing." But at this point in the game, what we are confronted with at night may not be very pleasant.

Nightmares are the first violent ring of the alarm bell. When nothing else has been able to make us pay attention, they are the last resort of our inner world; our night bullies attacking us to shock us into awareness. They flaunt our fears and angers in our face exactly as a neglected child flaunts bad behavior in front of his parents.

If we persist in neglecting our night child, he will become chronically bad, a repeat offender. Check back, do you have recurring dreams? Do you periodically dream that you miss your train, come unprepared for an exam or a speech, are lost, can't find your house, your car, lose your bag, are approached by a silent tramp, have your house broken into by an intruder, by a veiled figure, are beaten or handcuffed by two bullies (there are always two, representing duality), are faced with dirty toilets, seeping sewage and feces, bloodied meat, etc.

These are not very pretty images but they *are* your dreams. Are you going to disown them because you don't like their smell or the way they look? If you were to do that in your everyday world, your home and life would quickly become a mess.

What do all these dreams have in common? They are violent, oppressive, claustrophobic, dangerous, confusing, upsetting, disturbing, surrealistic, lonely, or simply too busy. Their colors are dark, dull, dirty, mixed, ranging from black and inflamed red to khaki and muddy, or they are artificial acid greens, intense yellows, glaring whites, blinding like neon or headlights.

Let me reassure you immediately—dreaming can be much more fun than this! But to each task its time. Your task now is to face yourself. This is your greatest challenge.

Will you be like the evil stepmother who looks into the mirror and expects to be told she is the most beautiful one of all? Or are you prepared to accept the truth? Can you make use of the mirror of your night dreams to show you your inner landscape, however unpleasant that might be? Knowing that "seeing" has its own safety net, and interacts with the dreams to shift and change their content, agree now to concentrate on your main task: remembering your dreams.

HOW TO REMEMBER YOUR DREAMS

"Forget your dream," says Cynthia's father at the beginning of this chapter. Many of us have done just that. We have learned to dim our inner vision, we have killed Merlin. You may protest that this has nothing to do with not wanting to "see"; you'd love to dream but you simply don't remember your dreams—in fact you think you *never* dream. But studies in sleep labs prove beyond a doubt that, at least during REM sleep, (rapid eye movement, detectable below the closed eyelids of a sleeping person) we *all* dream.

Search your memory, I am sure you will find at least one or two dreams, most probably unpleasant, but then isn't that why you originally forgot them? Wanting to avoid your unpleasant dreams does not mean you are a coward, but simply that you have a strong survival instinct.

It is time now to put to work some of what you have learned in this chapter about "seeing" the pattern of the dreams, even the unpleasant ones. Are you willing to take a look at your dreams? Are you willing to catch them, to try and hook them in in the same way that a fisherman drops a line and brings up treasures from the depths below?

If your answer is "yes," here's what you do.

Dream Book

Go out and buy yourself a blank notebook. Buy one you like. The nicer it is, the more convinced your dreams will be that you are interested in hearing from them. Bring your notebook home and open it to the first page. Write in it: "Dream Book." Put it on your night table next to your bed. Just before going to bed, open it to the next page, write at the top of the page that night's date, then leave the book open, and place your pen inside. You have now established your

intention to remember your dream. As you go to sleep, remind yourself that you want to remember your dream. It is useful at first to remind yourself to wake up at the time you have the dream so that you can catch it and write it down when it is fresh in your memory. If this doesn't work for you, write down your dream in your dream book in the morning. Record everything you remember, even if you think it is not important. Later you will see that your dreams know best what is important.

If you are going to write down a dream when you wake up in the morning it is essential that you give yourself a little time to do so before jumping out of bed. Relax into the same posture as when you were dreaming. This helps to stimulate your recall. Remember that dreams are elusive but also know that as you pay more attention to them they make themselves more available to you.

Perseverance is very important at this stage, as is having someone to tell your dreams to. Going through the process of telling a dream to someone almost always increases what you remember of it.

* * *

You may not like your dreams at first. You may find that your dreams are just too confusing, busy, or nondescript. You may recoil from your nightmares or your recurring dreams. Do not be discouraged. As you pay more attention to them they, like children, perk up, becoming cleaner, more alert, more focused, and more fun.

Soon you will find that you are thinking a lot about your dreams—you are wondering about the veiled woman or the locked drawer. These tantalizing children of your subconscious are inviting you to play with them. Roll up your sleeves like Hercules, and enter the game to play for all you're worth! The subject of the next chapter, interacting with the dream in your waking state, is your fourth task on the road to being a true dreamer and a master of the Life Plan.

A QUICK REFERENCE GUIDE TO CHAPTER 3 EXERCISES

Identifying Your Repetitive Behavior (p. 59)

Pay attention to repetitive postures, gestures, expressions, mimicry; words, sentences, jokes, stories; patterns of behavior.

Looking below the Surface: Locate an Area of Repetitive Failure in Your Life (p. 62)

Look below the surface to the source of failure. What image do you see? Breathe out once. Open your eyes.

Dream Book (p. 65)

Buy yourself a dream book and title it as such. Each night write the date in it and leave your Dream Book open on your night table, with a pen ready for you to write down your dream.

FOUR

Interacting with the Dream

"Good it is and good it may be (the bad dream). May the All-Merciful turn it to good; seven times may it be decreed from Heaven that it should be good and it may be good."

TALMUD, BERACHOT 55B

When dream images come crashing down on us like great birds of prey, crushing us to the ground, attacking our eyes, our guts, does it make good sense to dismiss them immediately as figments of our imagination, fabrications of our subconscious? When night comes and tidal waves menace, cars careen out of control, veiled figures haunt us, dark waters call, should we accept commonplace explanations that try to turn what are often distressing, painful experiences into cold metaphors or mere symptoms of half-formed physical, emotional, or mental states?

Suppose we do take these images seriously enough to write them down in our dream book and reflect upon them? Should we go along with them further, should we take seriously the implied danger they present to our bodies, to our very survival? And finally, having come this far, what do we do next? *The answer is that we have to give up being helpless bystanders to our dreams.*

Have you ever looked across a deep gorge and had a longing to leap across, but felt powerless in front of the wide chasm gaping at your feet? The chasm between your daytime life and your night life probably appears this way to you. At this point in your quest, daytime consciousness and sleep are still two vastly different and unrelated entities.

What do these terrifying dream images have to do with your daily life? You cannot judge them the same way you judge similar events in daytime consciousness. Sleep is veiled in mystery. Lethe, the river of oblivion, runs through your slumber even when you dream, and dreaming, too, can seem like a form of oblivion. What you retain of the night is not a clear moment of consciousness, but a memory of something elusive, something that possibly never was.

This elusive wisp of the subconscious that we call a dream may very well be fabricated by your imagination from the mere residue left by various bodily sensations you experienced during the night.

Or a dream might have manifested itself during REM sleep, but you cannot recall being present when it happened, at least not present in the same sense that you are present for the events of your daily life. More to the point, did the dream events actually happen in the dream the way you remember them happening? And if so, why did you not respond to them appropriately?

When we are awake, if we see a car careening toward us, we take the danger inherent in the situation seriously and jump aside in order to avoid the car. Why then, when dreaming, are we very likely *not* to react the same way and jump aside?

The answer is that, with a dream, we know it is possible to wake up and say, "Oh, thank God, that was only a dream!" But such scary dreams often come back. What if the dream won't go away? What if it persists in impressing upon us that danger is imminent and very real? What do we do? If we ignore the dream, should we not wonder what happens to our physical, emotional, and mental well-being when we are continually threatened with the shock of being hit by a car and then carry the terrible sense of anticipated impact and injury for days, weeks, maybe even years?

When a dream is very vivid and insists on being remembered, will reflecting on or talking about it help? Or is it possible to address a dream's demands for attention, what I call its "necessity," directly? Should we dream ourselves back into the dream and step out of the path of the careening car? Will doing this actually change anything?

Addressing what the dream wants you to address—its immediate necessity—may appear to be as crazy, perilous, and fraught with uncertainty as leaping over an abyss. When you make this leap toward the dream, you grant it enough gravity to hold you and yet, at the same time, you give up some of your secure knowledge with regard to what is real and what is imaginary. Thus, you take the risk of falling into an abyss of fantasy-making.

By answering the call of the dream, you are implying that you accept its reality, its "thingness." In that one leap, bridging the chasm between daytime consciousness and the night dream, you turn your worldview upside down. The implications are immense. Are you ready for this?

* * *

THE DREAM KNOWS BEST

Having now recorded a number of your dreams, when you read them over are you struck, as I am, by something obvious yet never mentioned?: the dream is always one step ahead of you. Like a good conversationalist, it invariably brings something new to the dialogue, illuminating some aspect of your life you haven't really paid attention to but which now needs your consideration. It warns you about pitfalls that are menacing, gives you previews of the coming attractions, presents events from the past in a new light, or simply reminds you of some subliminal message you have picked up but not registered consciously.

Your dream places itself solidly in front of you, adding something interesting, provocative, developmental, or growth-enhancing to the conversation. It never lags behind. And even when it appears to be repeating itself, its message is, "Hey, how many times must I say this until you finally pay attention and do something about it!?"

Imagine your subconscious as an ocean in whose depths events in your life have caused seismic upheavals. Now a tidal wave of emotional upset and physical shock is gathering, in your subconscious, to begin its journey to the surface of your consciousness. While you do not see into the depths of this ocean, it is a world your dreaming mind knows very well, a world your dreaming mind always tries to tell you about.

If the dream about the coming tidal wave is hopeful, you can get ready for better times. If it signals danger you can start heading to higher ground. The important thing in either case is to be able to read enough of the dream's pattern so that you can do *something*.

If you don't trust the reality of the dream, you will miss out completely. For example, if the dream was a joyful annunciation of hopeful tidings, you will not have anchored yourself in its hope. Or if the news was about trial and loss, you will not have prepared yourself properly and you will receive the full brunt of the painful event that the dream foretells. If you chose to do nothing, the tidal wave of emotion from the ensuing event will overpower you, only increasing your sense of help-lessness and stagnation. Given all this, don't you agree it is best to trust the dream?

Like Hermes, messenger of the gods, the dream comes on winged feet, harbinger of the new. It expects to be recompensed for its efforts. Will you respond, will you contribute something new to the dialogue?

THE POWER OF THE IMAGE

Not all dream images are harbingers of the future. As in daily life, where not every event moves us equally, many images in the dream pass without notice as part of the fabric of the dream's natural unfolding. But certain images can strike us like a hammer on an anvil. Once we have been exposed to them it is too late to pretend we haven't. We are like hot wax, imprinted with the marks of a great seal. If we don't stop ourselves from truly being present when these images happen, rever-berations can be as far-reaching, as intense and inexplicable, as falling in love at first sight.

However, whether we just react on the surface of our mind, or respond deeply with our whole being to the stimulation of these gener-ative images, is a matter both of temperament and of choice.

There is a Talmudic story about four rabbis who decided to visit the Garden of Eden (Talmud, Chagiagah 12a-b). Upon seeing its glory, the first rabbi died of shock, the second went mad, the third became an apostate. Only the fourth, Rabbi Akiba, went in and came out of the Garden unharmed and transformed.

What did all these rabbis except Rabbi Akiba have in common? All three *reacted* with shock, fear, disbelief, anger, rebellion: all negative emotions that can create "dis-ease" in our bodies. Only Rabbi Akiba *responded* to the *necessity* of what he experienced. Instead of reacting, he went in, "saw," and then returned to the everyday, workaday world (his *response*). How does one respond, instead of react?

When I was a child I often pondered the story of Saint Thomas Becket, the Archbishop of Canterbury who, while being murdered at his prayers by minions of King Henry II, had the strength to cry out, "Tell the king I forgive him!" Did he train himself not to react, I wondered?

Able to accept the inevitable, Becket found within himself what he needed to say: the only true words that would forever change the dialogue between himself and the king. How, in the spur of that horrible, violent moment, did Becket have the *heart* to adequately address the necessity of his situation, and respond instead of react?

REACTING TO OUR DREAMS

In our direst necessity at night, when the intruder breaks in, the bird swoops down, the dragon rises out of its muddy waters, the car careens and we are cornered, our survival instinct is prompted to wake us up. What better way to avoid danger, it seems, than to throw ourselves back into the conscious, waking world where images of the night cannot reach us.

If vampires disappear at the cock's crow, so do dreams upon awakening, or so we like to persuade ourselves. Of course, this change from one world to the other can go both ways. A terrible shock in this world can catapult us just as easily into the dream world. Like many a hero before us, we may find ourselves, while still awake, lost in a fog of confusion, indecision, delusion, fantasizing, vagueness, lack of awareness, a shutting down of our senses (not listening, not paying attention, etc.), vertigo, nausea, out-of-body sensations, hallucinations, paranoia, madness, coma.

These are not a pleasant list of potential consequences but, after all, they are a useful reminder that the arsenal of weapons from the dream world available for us to use against ourselves, if we choose to, is formidable indeed. Meanwhile, most people don't see that the consequences of shutting down our dreams are as harmful to us as what happens when we try to shut out the waking world.

When facing an awful reality (whether dream or waking) becomes too much for us to bear, we are used to simply opting out. Just as we often get trapped in the seesaw swing between reaction and instinct (see chapter 2), so too here we get caught in an oscillation between two locked-in poles.

Why not simply be present to what is presented to us and look necessity in the face? Why not face reality with the same determination, whether it is the reality of the dream or the reality of this world?

REASONS WHY WE WON'T FACE REALITY

If it were so easy to face reality, of course, I wouldn't be laboring this point. Being present in both worlds is the ultimate goal of the dreamer, a goal never achieved without very serious effort. So do not feel that you have failed when you opt for avoiding what you should be facing.

On the contrary, opting out is, in the short run, often the safest action you can take, for if you haven't been trained or equipped to face reality you are like a peasant alone in a field, being attacked by a huge knight on a horse. You have no horse, no armor, no sword, no lance, and no training. Sometimes the only thing you can do is run.

Opting out takes many forms, as the story about the rabbis illustrates. Most of us are like the rabbi who turned apostate, that is, we disbelieve our own eyes. Although we experience a dream as mysteriously alluring, we also may find its strangeness somewhat repellent. Without much practice at objective self-examination, we find it easy to distance ourselves from an experience that feels alien to us and to who we are.

It is easier to say "the dream *happened* to me" when what we really mean is "the dream is *not* me." In this way we can feel we are keeping a healthy distance between reality and the imagery that confronts us. Jumping over the abyss between them is just not our cup of tea.

But here's the rub: Despite what you say to yourself, the dream *is* you. You are its audience, yes, but you are also its author. You are not the victim of crazy images that are trying to muddle your head, you are their creator, the powerful, brilliant, imaginative, insightful, incisive creator of your dreams. This is the essential truth to hold on to if you start to get discouraged by the sometimes maddening elusiveness or unpleasantness of your dreams.

Remember that the place inside you where dreams are created is fundamentally optimistic and free. You can also begin to take heart from a very important corollary of being the maker of your dreams—you have the power to change them. But before you can regularly put this power to use, you must learn to truly claim your dream creations.

There are many ways people distance themselves from their dreams. As stated above, some people find it hard or distasteful to acknowledge a dream as their own creation. "I don't understand how I could have dreamed such a thing," they say. Or, "This is not me," or "I could never make up such a crazy scenario." Yet others go in an almost opposite direction, reacting to their dreams with superstitious awe. They see the dream as coming unadulterated and perfect from the furnace of their subconscious, or from some outside supernatural place.

For these people, just connecting a dream to their own interior life would ruin it for them, and to do anything as radical as to actually change a dream would be to destroy it entirely. Both types of people might consider that tampering with the dream's supposed message would be to topple into mere fantasizing.

Earlier we described how fantasizing easily becomes willful, self-indulgent manipulation of the Imagination (as discussed in the Introduction and chapter 1). It doesn't seem out of place to question whether changing our dream to fit our desires isn't an equivalent act of manipulation, a subtle or not so subtle distortion of the "true" dream as it issued from our subconscious. If we go back to a dream and transform ourselves from a ragged loutish peasant into a fierce young warrior fully clad and armed and ready to defend himself, are we not interjecting a lie into the dream landscape?

If returning to a dream does raise this legitimate anxiety for you, it could throw you off balance, like the rabbi who went mad. Or you may feel the ground is so slippery at this juncture where dreaming and willful intent meet, that it is best to kill off the dream altogether, like the rabbi who died of shock and, in this way, blocked out the vision completely. Or, like the third rabbi, you may decide that all this is "garbage" and walk away an unbeliever. Unfortunately, as the Talmudic sages remind us, "all dreams follow the mouth" (Talmud, Berachot 55:b). What you say about your dream will divert it toward your "interpretation." Rabbi Akiba's "interpretation" of the dream (wherein he and three other rabbis entered the Garden of Eden) was a peaceful one. Can we learn from Rabbi Akiba? Is there a more integral, safer way of approaching the whole matter?

THE HERO SHOWS THE WAY

Although we are given countless examples—in fairy tales, myths, and legends—of the successful way to face the necessity of our dreams, we still do not recognize the very helpful connection between myth and dreams for the simple reason that we haven't identified the hero: who he is, and where he comes from.

Who is the hero so altruistic and selfless as to battle with the black knight, kill the dragon, enter swamplands, walk through mirrors and fog, chop through walls of brambles or thick spider webs, descend into the underworld, face the dead, trick the monster? He is clearing the mirror of all the obstructions and muck, to find and rescue the lady, the land, or the cup. The lady, land, or cup is our pure body, our earth, our cauldron of plenty, our Garden of Eden, the womb that gives birth to all the wondrous beings, foods, and treasures of our dreaming.

The hero is our conscious mind.

He ventures into the dream world only upon being challenged by dire necessity or a haunting call. (A fierce dragon is devastating the land or a lady of surpassing beauty floats by holding a cup.) The hero is always male, that being the active principle, the volitional, intentional, sentient aspect of consciousness. He is young; this is his first foray into the dream world, the world where oblivion, forgetfulness, and slumber can overcome the unprepared traveler. He is untried; he has yet to face the wall of fog separating the two worlds, go through it, and remain conscious on the other side. He has yet to encounter the beasts that guard the entrance (his fears, angers, anxieties, greed, emotions that cloud the mirror) and subdue them, or trick them into allowing him through.

Will he be able to face the subconscious mind and not end up being sucked into unconsciousness? Will he be able to keep his consciousness bright and clear in the darkness? And if so, how does he do it?

THE FIRST STEP

The first step in this journey of bringing light into the darkness is accepting the challenge. When the car careens towards you, when the bird of prey swoops down upon you, this is the moment of your challenge. But of course you can't accept it, because you're asleep and you don't yet know how to be conscious in the dream state. That will come later.

How, then, are you going to face the challenge? You cannot do it while you are in the dream state, so you will do it from your position in this world, you will do it while conscious. Like a child who takes his first steps toward the water, you too must start on dry land because this is where you have been taught to be present and conscious. You begin your dialogue with the dream world while you are awake. Here is how.

You have been writing down your dreams. Take a look at the images that have struck you forcefully. What are they calling out for? Try to recognize what I have called their "necessity": what the dream is urging on you now. If a toilet is overflowing or a space is very black, you need to clean them. Don't ask, "Why me?" After all, this is *your* dream. Think of Hercules who had to clean the Augean stables. If a huge crane or tank is advancing towards you, you need to get out of the way!

If a veiled figure confronts you, you're being challenged to lift its veil. If a cave's black mouth gapes at you, or a fire-spitting dragon appears at your window, what are you going to do? Have you noticed that the challenges I have been presenting to you are progressively more difficult? Cleaning a toilet is distasteful but usually not dangerous, entering into a dark cave or facing a fire-spitting dragon is quite another matter.

Remember that fear is there to teach you courage. Without fear how would you know what courage is? How would you practice becoming courageous? Your first reaction to fear in a dream might be, "This is too ridiculous for words, I can't do this!" Or, "I'm terrified of even thinking about entering a dark cave!" Yet there was a time in your life when you practiced being courageous. There was a time when you were not afraid of being ridiculous, indeed, you had a great deal of fun imagining you were killing dragons or penetrating deep into the earth in search of treasures.

Then you were a child, just as Merlin (your seeing side now) is still a child. The hero is always young. When children are playing their imaginary games people think that they are pretending, but at this point you should be able to recognize that what they are doing is *very* real. They are practicing courage, they are teaching themselves how to confront reality, and both their intellect and their emotions—indeed their whole being—becomes involved in the play.

Safety in a dream world comes with being like a child. Yes, the child is frightened of the dragon at his window, but give him an imaginary arrow to shoot it with and he'll perk up and let fly the deadly dart, kill the dragon, and go right back to sleep!

Your hero side must play like a child. Just like a child, you can provide yourself with the necessary protection—the arrows, swords, shields, rifles, tanks, lights, ropes, and armies—that you need. Or you can arm yourself with trickery, like Perseus who, when he had to kill the Medusa whose face changed mortals into stone, turned the polished front of his shield upon her. When she saw her own reflection she turned to stone, enabling Perseus to cut off her head and use its fearsome power as a weapon to turn *his* enemies to stone.

All this is not new to you. You've read how heroes go about their tasks, you've been a child and played as fiercely as the rest of us. I'm simply reminding you that you can play again.

But how do you do it in your waking life?

Facing the Necessity of the Dream

Sit in an armchair with your arms and legs uncrossed. Close your eyes and breathe out three times very slowly, counting backwards from three to one, visualizing the numbers as you count them. See the number one as being tall, clear, and very bright. Then imagine that you arm yourself with all the protections and tools you think you may need and, returning to look at the particular dream image you want to deal with, proceed to answer its necessity. Attack the dragon with your lance or your arrows. Enter the cave with your powerful torchlight, your weapons. What do you find there and how do you deal with it?

Play for all you are worth. If you become afraid, you can always retreat and seek reinforcements (including finding a dream therapist who can guide you through this process). Remember, the child is always victorious.

HOW YOU KNOW YOU ARE VICTORIOUS

What happens as you play? The image you started with doesn't remain static. The dead dragon may transform into a bubbling brook, the cave reveal astonishing paintings. When your imaginal muscles respond to the dream's necessity, you are maintaining a dynamic contact with the original dream images while new dreaming starts flowing and a new image unfolds before your eyes. (If this doesn't happen it can mean that you are too frightened or otherwise reluctant to look at what is coming up, or you may just be concerned that you are fabricating the image). The new image that *does* appear may be a total surprise to you, it may call upon you to respond to its own new necessity.

In this manner each conscious dream takes you to a place where *that* dream's necessity is answered and a new configuration of dreaming offers itself to you. Thus you move as the clues are offered to you, exactly as you would in a treasure hunt.

If the clue says you must climb a high wall, you respond by producing a ladder. You are at play here, but for any real play to work, there have to be rules. The rule in conscious dreaming is that the process of going from one image to the next has to be kept open-ended. This means that you must let the dreams themselves control the story. They will tell you when you have reached the end of the treasure hunt.

If you follow this simple rule you will never have to worry about your will imposing itself on your dreams and warping them. As you can see, unless you give the dreams this freedom, all the fun and excitement of the hunt—finding each clue, deciphering its riddle, following its lead—will be lost to you. Letting dream images creatively appear this way is actually an easy and natural thing to do but, at first try, it may not *feel* easy and natural, causing you to fear you are *willing* the images to appear, or somehow "not doing it right."

Approach your practice with confidence, and don't hesitate to deal with the internal censor that says you are not seeing what you are seeing. Conscious dreaming is a skill that you get better at every time you do it, like swimming or dancing.

You will know you have found the treasure in your dreaming when, at some point in the flow of images, you experience a strong "aha!" feeling. You will suddenly feel very relaxed. You may have a floating sensation. Any new images will feel strong and comforting. As an old pattern moves into a new configuration, you will feel moved in your entire being. If you have effectively met the dream's necessity, your life can change in this world as well as in the dream world.

Contemplate doing this simple process by which being present and responding provides you—not only with the answer to what disturbs you—but also with the knowledge of how to transform and heal yourself.

Do I hear you accusing me of magical thinking? While it may seem that my thinking *is* magical, the dream reality, while not the same as our outer reality, is just as potent, and what happens in the dream reality is certainly real enough to make you feel differently. Once you experience its effects, you will begin to recognize its power.

When you venture as deeply into your dreams as I have been describing, how do you safely come back? Follow the example of Rabbi Akiba who knew to stay grounded when he was in the dream world so that, when it was time, he simply returned to *this* world.

Grounding Yourself

Breathe out from your diaphragm and ground yourself in the sensations of this world: sense your body in the chair, your back leaning against the backrest, your feet heavy on the ground, your hands weighted on the arm-rests. Then open your eyes and look around. As you reacquaint yourself with your body and your surroundings, retain the images and sensations of the new configuration of the dream. In this way you will not lose the experiences you ventured forth to gain.

Like Rabbi Akiba, you have successfully entered the glorious dream world, played your part, and successfully returned. Practice this movement until it feels perfectly comfortable to you. In your fifth task, you will begin a different movement. Instead of providing your dream hero with the weapons of the waking world, you will have the help of the Lady, the dream voice, and you will use her unusual weapons in this, your conscious waking world.

A QUICK REFERENCE GUIDE TO CHAPTER 4 EXERCISES

Facing the Necessity of the Dream (p. 77)

Identify the necessity of your dream. Then close your eyes, and breathe out three times, counting backwards from three to one, visualizing the numbers as you count them. Return into the dream and, arming yourself with the protections and tools you need, face the dream image you want to deal with.

Grounding Yourself: Learn to Ground Yourself When You Return from the Dream World: (p. 79)

Pay attention to your sensations: your feet on the ground, your hands heavy on the armrests of your chair, your back against the backrest, your buttocks sinking in the chair. Breathe out once. Open your eyes and be aware of all your sensations while, at the same time, with open eyes visualize your dream images.

FIVE

Reversing

"Return to me and I will return to you."

MALACHI 3:7

It is not without reason that we associate *all* dreaming with the dreaming that happens when we are asleep. Yet it is actually in the twilight zone between sleep and awareness, when we are reclining, relaxed, and abandoned, that we "re-member" our dreaming. (Later we will see how we can also train ourselves to become aware of dreaming while we are deeply asleep or wide-awake and upright.) It is when our eyes have wandered out of focus that we daydream; when half-asleep that we are flooded with hypnagogic images (see chapter 1).

Those vivid, disparate images wash up to our semi-closed or closed eyelids like waves onto a beach. We still retain our consciousness when we witness these images, but we are on the brink of losing it. As soon as we sink into sleep, the waters close over us, separating us from our conscious mind. And for most of us the night passes in oblivion. It is only as our slumber lightens and we come closer to awakening that we remember some images from our dreams.

What of our young hero, Conscious Mind Courageous? He has set out to conquer the oblivion of sleep. Is he making an impossible challenge when he rides out against the black knight that guards the dream world and its mysteries? He has only his sword with which to battle against nothingness, and the sharp weapons of consciousness cannot penetrate that particular wall.

This time the hero cannot attempt to solve the problem as he did in chapter 4 by bringing the dream into the waking world. This time he must face the dream's necessity on the dream's own ground. He is in great danger of failing, for he has no weapons against sleep.

But as he is about to collapse into oblivion—or, in the imagery of the Arthurian cycle, lose his head to the black knight—Merlin, our "seeing" self, appears by (our) Arthur's side to remind him (us) that if he just *comes close* to the still waters of sleep, and pays attention, he will be granted another weapon.

See, just now a sword is thrust out of the waters by a milky white hand! The Lady of the Lake, ruler of the dreaming waters, has stretched her arm up through the veil and offers Arthur, not the warm enfolding of an embrace, but an astonishing weapon for him to grasp. What does this dream sword signify?

We think of consciousness as sword-like, incisive, and judging. Is there an acuity to dreaming? Is there a form of dreaming consciousness we can lay hold of which cuts through the illusions of the everyday world? The hero is proffered a "dreaming sword." How does he grasp it and wield it in the everyday world? If we, like him, learn to seize the sword and become its wielder and master, how will we benefit?

* * *

REVERSED WORLDS

There is nothing more slippery than a dream. You think you have it pinned down, but then it vanishes into thin air and you are left with nothing but a nagging need to recapture the dream, a longing to submerge yourself once again in its embrace. There is no "real" veil, fog, or darkness in your mind that you can blame the disappearance of the dream on, it's just that the minute you wake up, the screen where your dream was starts to go empty and then usually becomes totally blank as your mind rapidly fills with thoughts of the new day ahead of you.

The moment when you can still catch your dream images is so short-lived that it is easy to fear that you may never be gifted with the dream sword. Have you ever tried to seize the exact moment when day becomes night, or when the first light of dawn appears in the darkness? As the sun starts to rise, before you know it, you have lost the darkness and are looking at shapes that weren't there a moment ago! Or at sunset, you lose the shapes that were visible only a moment before, as you are plunged into darkness.

To help you feel more confident about being able to consciously reach your dreams, let's play a game.

Shifting Positions

Stand before a mirror. As you gaze at your image, let yourself become that person in the mirror. You have geographically changed places and are standing in the mirror, looking out at the real you (beyond the mirror). Now shift from being in the mirror and, as you continue gazing, become aware of being in your body as usual. Do this several times while you notice how you feel.

Is this fun, or is it a little eerie? Do you lose yourself easily, or is it difficult and new for you? Even if you think you have never played this game before, like dreaming itself, you did it naturally when you were young, and you do it now whether you are aware of it or not.

Becoming more aware of this shift will help you become more adept at catching the moment when you shift from consciousness to sleep and from sleep back to consciousness. You will see that it is only by consciously experiencing the shift that you may be able to trick the dream world into giving up its sword and the secrets attached to it.

Your dreaming self is like your twin image when you enter the mirror. What you feel when you identify with your mirror image is what dreaming is all about. Dreaming is the reverse of conscious embodiment. In the same way as darkness is defined by light and light by darkness, so dreaming and consciousness define each other. Like the Dioscuri, the twins Castor and Pollux, sons of Leda but each twin having a different father, (Pollux's father was the god Zeus, Castor's father was Tyndareus, a mortal), these two versions of ourselves stand for our heaven and our earth.

Whereas our conscious mind (earth) is active, focused, thrusting, willful, incisive, cutting, separating, judging, our dreaming mind (heaven) is laid back, relaxed, receptive, passive, flowing, accepting, wide, and all-encompassing. Whereas the conscious mind seizes, directs, proceeds linearly and by elimination, the dreaming mind dissolves, transmutes, leaps ahead or in any which direction—like the all-powerful queen in the game of chess.

In dreaming, everything is possible; shapes assemble and transform like clouds in the sky. In the conscious world we pit ourselves against defined obstacles and strive to conquer them so that we may grow. Limitations suppose density, weight, time. In the dream world there is no density or weight or time. There may be obstacles, but our striving is *of the moment.*

Imagine a huge boulder blocking your path. With a flick of your dream finger you can make that boulder roll away, just as a gust of wind will make a cloud disperse. In the dream world, change is instantaneous, its freedom enchanting. What, then, is its sword?

THE SWORD OF DREAMING

The dream sword works for your conscious mind the way the fisherman's hook worked for your dream mind in chapter 3. There, when the elusive dream image bites, your conscious mind tackled it and pulled it into full consciousness in order to fix it in its memory or its dream book.

How does the sword work? In accordance with the laws of the dreaming world (relaxation), the sword lies back, flat like water (reversing), and offers its shiny surface for contemplation (mirroring). The instant you peer into its liquid mirror, the image you are searching for is thrust upon you, its truth unadorned and unembellished, as piercing as a sword.

Beware that the image you encounter is your response to looking within, so it belongs to you as "your image." The inner world it comes from can present you with an image of your face, but it can also provide any of the sensory manifestations of the inner world. This can mean a voice, a smell, a texture, a taste, a visual shape, or all of these in any combination. The next instant, after becoming aware of it, of course, you may erase or change the image to suit your vanity or your expectations. But if you do this, you run the risk of derailing into fantasy instead of staying on the main track in your search for the truth.

For, you see, the truth has been outed in that first encounter, like a jack-in-the-box that pops up in front of your face when you least expect it. Trying to force it back into the box will not change it. You have "seen," and the seed of truth has impregnated you.

The dream sword is your truth. Like a good dueler, it uses surprise to catch you off guard. It attacks where you are most vulnerable. Touché! In one instant all is changed, you have been touched! Maybe your dream image faced you with another you, one more stingy or more guilty than you want to believe possible, or maybe, in your dream, you were given an answer, different than the one you wanted to hear, to a question that you have been wrestling with.

As soon as you turn your senses inward, like a mirrored reflection, your truth stares back at you, sometimes so shocking in its impact you feel the stab in your heart, but sometimes also so low-key that you don't register its wounding until later. Then we call its intimations "intuition," or "the inner voice."

Either way, do you think you can escape your truth's luminous insight? You can disown what is offered to you in that first instant, or you can convince yourself you didn't really "see" it. This is easy since, like all dream fragments, the message won't linger long. It must succeed in making a strong "impression" on you in that one instant. If it doesn't do this, it will either leave you feeling pregnant with a nagging feeling that there is something you should be paying attention to, or it will dissolve and disappear from your consciousness.

You can look again, hoping to get a different message, but the dream knows its questioner and this makes it tricky to ask the same question twice. More than likely, if you do so, it will accommodate you with a fantasy image. In the end, you can always go back to change or manipulate the image to suit your false conceptions about yourself. You are the dream maker after all, and willy-nilly the creator of its story. Even if you distort the dream, these distortions have your signature. Every pattern unfolding before you on the surface of the mirror is you.

However, refusing the first impressions from this mirror will make the process much more laborious. The fantasy image you choose instead spirals you off, away from your truth, into a cul-de-sac which is the *opposite* of truth. From here, eventually, you will have to disentangle the truth at the cost of much pain, effort, and time, plus all the regrets that go with knowing that you could have listened to your "inner voice" in the beginning. Sooner or later, the thrust of the dream sword is inescapable.

KNOW THYSELF

At the same time that truth is best for us, it is also a dangerous commodity few of us can handle with serenity. Only a youth, a fool, or a would-be hero, reckless or bold enough to want to tear the veil asunder, will accept the challenge of the black knight who guards the waters of sleep and the Lady who owns them.

To battle him is to risk being felled by the insight he guards. An example of this is the young Luke Skywalker in *Star Wars* who, after chopping off the head of his dark enemy finds himself, to his horror, face-to-face with himself.

Another example is the Greek god Perseus. He is wiser than Skywalker because, equipped with helpful instructions from the gods, he does not look directly at the deadly face of Medusa before he cuts off her head. Thus he avoids being petrified by the blinding truth of his own "monstrosity."

After cutting off the head of Medusa, Perseus throws it into a black bag, thereby cloaking the Lady's awesomely dreadful beauty. Perseus plays hide-and-seek with the truth, just as Adam and Eve did with God after tasting of the fruit of good and evil. For, like that famous fruit, truth to us is both good and evil and must be handled with care.

Black bag, black knight, slumber, oblivion, our blindness . . . like a black cloth veiling the mirror in a house of mourning, the lady's fearsome protector also serves to protect *us*, guarding us from the too startling, too painful, too terrifying truth. Who would wish to lift the veil of his own blindness without having some form of protection?

We must come to the truth layer by layer. As a Talmudic story tells us, if we were to peel an onion to its core in one night, the next morning we would be dead. No one can look suddenly upon the face of God (in whose image we are made) and live. How then can we train ourselves to lift the peels one by one, layer by layer, slowly and with care, with regard for our own vulnerability and self-worth? How do we make friends with the truth?

THE LADY'S OFFER

Although the truth may appear to us to be horrifying, terrifying, evil, or too good to be true, it is only in our eyes that this is so. The truth is what it is, neither good nor bad, just a mirror reflection of what is inside of us. It is no enemy to us, only to the plethora of our desires, expectations, vanities, and fears, whose infantile willfulness veils our access to the mirror and distorts its true image.

Clearly the Lady wishes us well. That her realm is Binah, the sphere of discernment, (the third sphere in the kabbalistic Tree of Life), may surprise us, for we associate the feminine with all things sweet, tender, and loving. Discernment, on the other hand, is slightly distant, cool, appraising. It is in the Lady's offering of discernment that the sword's power is freed. But she does not give it as an aggressive challenge to us. It is a gift, whether or not we are still too untested to recognize it as such. Truth, when we are ready to receive it, is like honey.

In fact, the Lady is so far from being an enemy that she offers the hero her sword when his is split in two battling the black knight. For him to take the sword he must travel across the waters of sleep to the white hand that holds it out to him.

"You can have my sword if you become the water and the hand that holds it," she seems to be saying. Is this a trick? If he *becomes* the water he will be sucked into its darkness. Merlin, our young, imaginative "seeing" aspect, is standing by, always available when we wish to consult him, to show the hero the simple way—a boat hidden in the reeds by the water's edge, its hull rounded like a chalice or an embrace, another gift from the dream lady. How does he step into the boat and, enclosed in its cocoon, glide safely across the abysmal waters?

Easy! You are now aware of the reverse nature of the dream world. You know how shifting feels. Why not trick sleep by anticipating the shift, by consciously shifting into sleep's position? At the twilight zone where consciousness and sleep meet, lay back in your bed, as if in the hull of a boat, and allow yourself to become the dreaming one, knowingly watching from your prone position as consciousness peers into your mirror.

Sink into the physical postures of dreaming: you are reclining, relaxed, eyes closed. Think the opposite of erect, poised to move, eyes open. By knowingly adopting the dreaming stance, you are luring your conscious self back into the dreaming, just as your mother, when you were an infant, by her touch, voice, and prompting, lured your dreaming self into consciousness.

Watch as consciousness, from its point in time—this very moment when you are still awake, just before slipping into sleep—is funneled into your dreaming self like a whirlpool. Being actively receptive, you as your dreaming self know yourself (I use "knowing" in the Biblical sense of fully embodied experiencing) to be faithfully reflecting back to your conscious mind its own unfolding, which is rewinding, like a tape, from this moment in time back to its starting point in the morning when you woke up to the daily world.

As consciousness pours itself back into you, see yourself as the apprentice of the goddess Nut, the Egyptian goddess of the sky who, each night swallows the sun into her dark embrace, annihilating in her darkness everything that is not of essence, catching as in a sieve the gold nuggets of the day's experiences. In so doing you have tricked yourself outside of the all-too-familiar "conscious you," back into the goddess's arms. You have become this other self watching you, your twin. Your experience of the "conscious you" has moved from its original position as a separating, distinguishing, objectifying, dichotomizing awareness to an experiential, all-encompassing, self-accepting, dreaming knowingness.

Reversing

Try this in bed tonight. Turn off the lights, lie down, close your eyes, and relax totally while watching yourself relax. When you feel either very heavy or so light you are almost floating, begin looking at your day backwards. As you watch, allow what you see to sink in without judgment or commentary, simply recognizing it for what it is. Just before turning off the light, were you reading a book? See yourself doing that, acknowledge all the thought forms that came along with your reading. Before coming to bed did you brush your teeth? Rewind the tape: coming to bed, leaving the bathroom, brushing your teeth. Recognize the sensations and thought forms that came with brushing your teeth. Move back through your day's activities. When you come to that difficult encounter you had with your teenage son on the stairs, (your wife, your boss. . .) you are no longer confronting him, you (your dreaming self) are seeing you from outside as you interact with him. To fully comprehend the experiential value of reversing and

shifting positions, use your dreaming freedom. Imagine that you go and step into the shoes of the person you are confronting, taking his exact geographical position. You'll now get a view of yourself as he sees you. At this moment he/you serves as your dreaming mirror. You will see, from his viewpoint, how you looked, how you moved, how you behaved, and how you sounded to him.

You have never seen this before because you were so busy being you, the conscious one, fixated on presenting a solid identity to the world. Now you are being instructed by your dreaming self who, as free and light-footed as the flamboyant queen of the medieval world of chess, can move to any position it fancies to get a better reflection of the truth.

You are *experiencing* the truth, not judging it. As you experience it, the essence of what needs to be learned from the experience will sink into you and make an impression. We call this exercise "Reversing" or the "Exam of Conscience Backwards." It brings about what the kabbalists call *Tshuva* which is often translated as repentance, but which really means "turning" away from, allowing us therefore to face a new perspective.

DETACHMENT AS A DREAMING MANEUVER

Now tell me, once you have tried it, isn't it easier to be holding the dream sword than to be shocked and afflicted by its wounding? The legend tells us that the hero who takes up the dream sword and wears its scabbard receives another and not inconsiderable gift: he no longer bleeds from the wounds inflicted upon him. Now that he is in the dreaming position, he experiences the truth as simply what it is. He has learned to "see" with all the detachment that distance and the viewpoint from another world can give him.

But isn't the act of detachment generally deemed an intellectual maneuver, the ability of consciousness to distance itself and objectify? Stepping out of the subjective, all-sensing experience of darkness into the light is an Apollonian prerogative. Consciousness sits on a throne apart, like Solomon dispensing justice, in the image of God who separated heaven and earth, night and day, the waters from the land . . . *Je pense, donc je suis,* ("I think, therefore I am.")

Yet were you aware that Descartes wrote this famous aphorism, establishing an objective philosophical foundation for scientific inquiry, after he first heard the phrase in a *dream*? If dreaming can also bring distancing, what is the difference between this dreaming detachment and conscious objectification?

Behold the goddess Nut. Her body is like a great ark filled with stars. She does not objectify, she merely considers. As the Latin root of this word tells us, "com" + "sidereal" means "at one with the stars." Spread out, they scatter their light over our dichotomies; dome-like, Nut arches over both stars and us, enfolding and dissolving our difficulties in her healing darkness.

Think of it! Dreaming, like the dragonfly, can position itself anywhere and, at the same time, on all the points on the circumference of a sphere, including—to better experience its focal point—at the center of the sphere. Because of its great mobility, dreaming allows us to consider from the unnumbered viewpoints of the stars.

As becomes clear from Descartes' experience with dream and scientific inquiry, consciousness and dreaming need each other, just as night and day cannot exist one without the other. While consciousness will straddle dreaming to leap from subjectivity to objectivity, dreaming straddles consciousness to knowingly hold, within its wide gaze, our many ambiguities, transmuting them into a living world of paradox.

PRACTICE

My teacher Colette used to say that if you practice Reversing for seven years each night without fail, you need no other instruction to become enlightened. (You will then be living in the spiritual light which is beyond night and day, beyond all dichotomies, with the two worlds having become one within you.) If you take up the dream sword, you take possession of a mighty weapon to dissolve your daily illusions and contradictions. Therefore practice, practice, practice!

At first you will probably fall asleep before you have remembered no farther back than when you left the bathroom. (Working on reversing is an excellent, drugless remedy for insomnia!) Then, as you are able to reverse farther back in your day, you will be assailed by intense boredom. When you examine the past, you will discover that it is hard to give up habits of judgment and recrimination.

Then, as you overcome boredom, you will begin to find yourself illumined by the many gold nuggets of insight caught in your dreaming net. Continue, and do not be enticed even by them. One day, you will find yourself reversing during the *daytime*, exactly as some violent confrontation is about to erupt between you and your teenage son (or your wife, or your boss).

Touché! You have caught the instant in a life situation when you are about to forget yourself, and therefore lose your ability to choose your actions and be pulled helplessly into blind instinctual or reactive behaviors, which are simply other forms of psychological oblivion or busyness.

Think, for example, how sleep or consciousness can blindly pull you away from your hard-won images of truth, into either oblivion or busyness. Whenever you can consciously use your dreaming self in the living moment, you have reached a moment of truth, a pause that makes it possible for you to make choices. Will you decide to go down the habitual path or will you take "the one less traveled"? Can you say "no" to oblivion and busyness?

* * *

You are back where you started, wiser by far, but still face-to-face with the black knight. You have the promise of the dream sword, but before you engage in battle again wouldn't it be a good idea to know as much about your instinctual world—your enemy the black knight—as you can? Who is he? How does he move? How does he fight? Can you unmask him? That will be your sixth task.

A QUICK REFERENCE GUIDE TO CHAPTER 5 EXERCISES

Shifting Positions (p. 83)

Stand before a mirror. As you gaze at your image, let yourself become that person in the mirror. Geographically, perceive yourself in the mirror looking out at the real you outside the mirror. Shift back to being in your body as usual. Do this several times.

Reversing (p. 88)

This is one of your key practices. Do it every night without fail. Do it in bed, with your eyes closed, just before going to sleep: Look at your day backwards, as if rewinding the tape of your day. When you come upon a difficult encounter with someone, go stand in that person's shoes. Look at yourself from that person's vantage point. When you see clearly how you were behaving, return to your body and continue reversing the day's events.

SIX

Returning to Your Senses

"My master [the Baal Shem Tov] revealed to me that when a person has pain, whether physical or spiritual, he should meditate that even in his pain, God can be found. He is only concealed in a garment in this pain. When a person realizes this, then he can remove the garment. This pain and all evil decrees can be nullified."

TOLDOT YAAKOV YOSEF

Each day the sun sinks below the horizon, plunging the world into darkness. Each day our bodies are also pulled into the darkness, our senses eventually switching off like snuffed candles. Who tells us to shut down? Like sheep, our bodies follow that great shepherd in the sky. Our consciousness, its Apollonian pride conquered, fades away. Lulled into quietude, we are felled by the hidden enemy—the black knight envelops us in his garb.

Uncompromising, unpitying, unswerving in his intent, he uses his one weapon—instinct—to conquer us. We can wrestle him, refuse to be extinguished, or stay up all night, but he comes back, stronger than our intent. Sooner or later, whether it is day or night outside, the sun in our mind turns off, the darkness rises, and we are conquered.

Who is this anonymous other who not only seals off our consciousness in sleep, but acts as a "reducing valve" to lock out of our awareness many of the signals that otherwise bombard us at every instant?

What creates an ocean's tides, its waves, its stormy darkness or lustrous flatness? The relative attractions of sun, moon, earth, the seasons,

93

and the weather, of course. But who orders the ocean to move and change in the many ways it does? No one. The ocean follows the interconnected actions of gravity, wind, temperature, seismic shifts.

So too our body follows nature's universal laws as it sucks in air and throws it out, pumps blood through its veins, breaks down its food so it can be absorbed and assimilated by different organs, and continually collects and eliminates the many wastes that result from the body's energy-producing metabolism.

Who tells the body what to do? No one or, if that someone exists, their presence is deeply hidden in the physical subconscious. Fixed in its own regularity like a beast yoked to a revolving wheel, the autonomic nervous system orders the simple motor activities and instincts that keep us alive.

Try to pin it down, throttle it, smother it, and it kicks back with a vengeance. Breathing, eating, sleeping, moving; these are the things that rule us. *Chassez le naturel, il revient au galop!* ("Chase away what is natural, it gallops back!") say the French, who have a healthy appreciation for the pleasures that the beast side of us provide.

Like Osiris, the Egyptian god of the Underworld who was tricked by his evil brother Seth into climbing into a coffin that was then sealed shut upon him, our spirit has been tricked into the coffin of our physicality. Our animal body, the beast who serves us with dog-like devotion, paradoxically becomes our jailer. Who will free us from its confining clutches? What hero or heroine, prodded by what necessity, will snatch us from the darkness of our instinctual body?

* * *

DISMEMBERMENT

On the calm surface of things, the autonomic movements of our bodies seem regular, predictable, unchanging. The body, like all animals, is a creature of habit. It knows only the regular ticking of its internal clocks, themselves regulated to the clocks of the universe.

Chinese acupuncturists have observed one of these clocks for every organ in the body: the heart, the lungs, the intestines, the kidneys, the spleen. Each organ has its own specific rhythm; each reaches its peak activity or sinks to its lowest ebb at a different, fixed moment of the day's twenty-four hour cycle. If the body is your Earth and each organ a different country around the globe, when darkness falls on the intestines the sun will rise on the lungs. Thus, in the course of the body's daily revolution around the sun, each organ experiences its noon and its midnight and, in the course of the yearly revolution, its rise and fall of seasons.

Its seeds—the cells—are born, grow, multiply and die, to be replaced by other cells. Every seventh year, (the end of another great cycle), all the cells in the body finally die and are replaced by new cells. Traversing the trajectory of its life from beginning to end, like the constellations in the night sky, the body passes through its fixed asterisms: conception, birth, growth, adulthood, decline, and death, exactly as a tree does from seed, to young sapling, to full adulthood, to loss of foliage, and finally death.

Exactly so was the great god Osiris reduced, (at the hands of his brother Seth, god of limitations) to nothing more than a physical body and sent floating down the birth canal. As Osiris journeyed down the Nile, entombed in his physicality, the tree of his earthly body grew around him, so perfect and strong that the king of Byblos, happening upon it, set it up as the central column and spine of his palace in Byblos.

There Osiris would have remained were it not for Isis: his wife, sister, twin, and beloved, with whom Osiris dreamt and made love in the womb. Even in Osiris's death-trance, we feel the pain of his separation from Isis, obscure and heavy as that of a dumb beast. But who is she really?

It is Isis who comes seeking Osiris, she who tricks her way into the palace of his body to be near him and, awakening him, brings him back to Egypt. However, brother Seth soon is up to his old, evil tricks and, discovering the return of Osiris, cuts his brother's body up and disperses it to the winds. Now again, Isis must reclaim Osiris who, blind to her presence, deaf to her calls, and dismembered into fourteen different body pieces, (all ticking at different times), has blanked out his partner.

Isis finds Osiris again and "re-members" his missing body parts (which were scattered all over the land) in order to resurrect his creative powers.

Like so many Sleeping Beauties, we too are locked into the Osirian myth. Just as the straw man needs a brain, the tin man a heart, the lion courage, we too need our Wizard of Oz to grant us what we already have but have forgotten we had: the freedom to fly, transform, click our heels, and be wherever we choose instantly. Isis is our wizard, our earth-mother, our dream Lady. She alone can enliven our darkness and resurrect our freedom. But what activates her, if we can't, since we, by definition, are asleep?

PAIN'S GUIDANCE

How can a car move when there is no driver to turn the key that will spark the ignition? It can't, obviously, but eventually its empty seat attracts a driver. So it is with Isis; Osiris's oblivion is her call. Her longing to spark the ignition serves as a bridge back.

Her pain at the loss of her playmate guides her, as it guides all the great goddesses and heroes who suffer the Fall into the natural order: Demeter to search for Persephone; Orpheus for Euridice; Adam and Eve for the lost Garden of Eden—as it guides *us* also, and prods us, electrifies us—to search the underworld of our pain. Pain is our guide, the shock that disrupts the natural order of things.

Yet have you noticed? At first, pain blurs perception. When in pain we tend to blot out the world, sink back into an instinctual stupor. Where, then, is the promised insight brought on by pain? The black knight still stands, unchallenged. Will pain be our downfall or can it become our Perceval and save us? In pain we are still operating within the black knight's dominion, the instinctual mode, (breathing, eating, moving, touching, seeing, hearing, sleeping), but pain breaks through the instinctual mode's dull monotony, perturbing its rhythm.

When an ocean is hit by a major earthquake it continues to engage in wave formations but, in great excess of what is habitual, the waters recede far out to sea then rise to tsunami height. In the same way, when we are smitten with pain—physical, emotional, or even mental—our rhythms change drastically, ruffling our black knight's composure. Our breathing becomes shallow, our appetite is compromised, we curl up in bed in a fetal position in the middle of the day. We protect ourselves by sinking into an excess of instinctual behavior.

While the black knight appears to be victorious, both the highs and the depressions of our behavior alert Isis to the need for rescue. How does she act to prevent us from succumbing to the blind forces of the body?

THE DREAM LADY'S DOUBLE STRATEGY

As always, the way in is simpler than we think. In fact, it is child's play! Isis, mistress of her dreaming, seeks out not the adults, the jaded ones, but the children; her little helpers with the roaming eyes and playful curiosity. Sure enough, they have "heard" and "smelt" the rumors of Osiris' passage, they have "seen" his coffined body floating down the river towards Byblos.

Untrammeled by thoughts or doubts, they display—first strategy—the alacrity and inventiveness to turn their senses inwards. Having lit upon the trail laid out for us by Nature, they guide Isis in, reminding her to improvise—second strategy—as she goes along, to playfully grapple with and respond to whatever she encounters.

How can we, like them, catch sight of the fallen stars caught fast in the mesh of our nature and follow them to their source, there to awaken the power of our imagination? For here is the conundrum: Imagination lies deeply hidden within our nature, somewhere below our instincts, in the underworld of our subconscious.

In our nature, in the Osirian darkness, lie the seeds of inspiration, the sparks of light that need gathering and igniting by the "seeing" child in us, for us finally to vanquish the black knight. Take heart, this is simpler than you think. Are you ready?

RETURNING TO OUR SENSES

See life and its trials as a pure stream rushing down from the mountaintops, and think of stepping into it with bare feet and, walking up against its current, returning to its source. There you will find and drink of the pure waters of Imagination and be refreshed.

Just so does Isis journey against the current of her pain that would rush her down to the vast, undifferentiated ocean. She is propelled by longing for the source, guided by a smell of freshness, the sound of a murmur, the gurgling of a spring.

Overwhelmed by the forces of Nature, spilled forth into an unconscious traveling stream, Osiris is unknowing of Isis' proximity. Her senses, her seeing, her smelling, her hearing guide her, opening the way and moving her forward. They are the servants she consorts with near the palace of Byblos, the devoted ones she knows can lead her in.

So too, guided by our pain to travel to its source, are we brought into the palace by our servants, our senses. Would you like to try?

Seeing a Physical, Emotional, or Mental Pain

Close your eyes. Breathe out three times, counting from three to one, seeing the numbers clearly. See the number one as being tall, clear, very straight, and very bright. Now become aware of a pain in your body. It can be a physical, emotional, or mental pain. Just locate its place in your body. Then imagine turning your eyes inward and traveling down to the source of your pain. "See" it with your inner eyes. How does it appear to you? What color is it? Does it smell? Does it have a texture? Is it hot or cold, inflamed or dull, wet or dry? Describe everything you "see" about your pain. In "seeing" it, your imagination becomes true to its source.

As it "sees," the necessity of its "seeing" will impel your imagination to do something about what it "sees." For instance, your pain may be very red, wet, and inflamed. How can you deal with its necessity? Like the children, improvise! For instance:

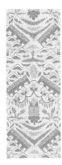

Mopping Up an Inflammation

Breathe out three times. Imagine that with a pure white cotton wad you mop up the red inflamed wet color until it permeates the cotton. Then take the cotton and throw it over your left shoulder. There, it is gone! When you look again, the area of your old pain looks clear and light. The pain is gone. Breathe out and open your eyes.

In this exercise you remember your body as your imagination's blueprint conceives it: clear, healthy, filled with light.

REMEMBERING YOUR BODY

Now that you know that, as Blake put it, "the Eternal Body of Man is the Imagination. . .God himself, the Divine Body" and that "we are his members," are you not tempted to resurrect not just one dying part but the whole, perfect body such as Imagination gave to us? Are you not compelled, like Isis, to search for all the fourteen parts of the god's scattered body and to re-member him? Or are you too afraid of pain, preferring to lull it to sleep?

Instead, can you think of pain not so much as a disruption but as a blessing? As the opening of the way in to unbelievable new insights, new possibilities, new life? Can you see your way to welcoming any form of disruption as the opportunity for you to see and to re-awaken, within the flaws of the physical body, the perfect body of your imagination?

It is you and you alone who can do this work, as it was Isis, and only Isis, who could find and identify each of Osiris' members. Each time you experience a pain, a disruption, it is not in your mind that it first appears, but in your body. Under attack, your body contracts, agitates, collapses. Your brain fires many more neurons than is its wont.

Therefore, lose no time in returning back to the exact locality of the pain in your body. Explore it, "see" it, and do for it what needs doing. As you become adept at this work, you will not only identify your pain before it lulls you into blind behavior, you will also be bringing into illumination more of the perfect body Blake speaks of. But can you illuminate your body completely?

Isis, tirelessly searching for the fourteen members of her husband's body, found all but one. The phallus, member of regeneration, was missing. Using her imagination and the god Toth's knowledge (his claim to godhood), she fashioned a perfect phallus of gold, gold representing the binding of knowledge and creativity, the alchemical stone.

Straddling Osiris' erect member, she conceived Horus, the perfect child. We too, if we pursue with alacrity and inventiveness an exploration of our physical body, will bring to life the perfect child in us, our imagination. This is not difficult to do. Only lethargy stands in the way. Push lethargy off to the left and begin your work.

Visiting Your Body

Close your eyes. Breathe out three times, counting from three to one, seeing the numbers clearly. See the number one as being tall, clear, very straight and very bright. Now decide to visit one of your body "members." Decide, for instance, to visit the index finger of your right hand. Turn your eyes inward, imagine them traveling down your arm into your index finger. Now you are looking at the inside of your finger. What do you sense and "see"? Is it hot, cool, cold? Is it dry or wet? Is it dark or light? What color is it? Is an image attached to it? (Such as, for example, a table and chairs sitting in your finger). Breathe out once. As you continue to look at your inside index finger, what are you sensing in your finger? What is happening to your habitual way of perceiving it? Is it smaller or bigger or the same size? Is it wider or narrower or the same width? Is it still dense, dark, or is it becoming lighter? Translucent? Open your eyes. How does your inner "seeing" of your finger differ from your habitual outer perception of it?

I will not tell you how I or others perceive the differences, for I would not influence your "seeing." Suffice it to say that the inner and outer perceptions are radically different. Continue practicing this exercise, visiting each "member"' of your body, applying yourself to its reality. Soon you will begin to "see" the transfigured body, the True Body of the Imagination.

Like the risen Christ in the Grunewald triptych, or like the illuminated body which is said to materialize before the eyes of the initiated kabbalist, it glows with your "seeing," it shines with the light of the senses you have turned in to bear upon it. By "seeing" your body this way, you will have pierced through the darkness thrust upon you by the black knight. Straddling and in control of the boar (the wild pig) of your darkest instincts, like luminous Horus, you are ready for your next task.

* * *

Your next task takes you into battle with Seth, your limitations. Now that you have given birth to your imagination, you have its playful power at your command. Your seventh task will be to explore the thousand and one different ways of pushing your limits.

A QUICK REFERENCE GUIDE TO CHAPTER 6 EXERCISES

Seeing a Physical, Emotional, or Mental Pain and Mopping It Out of Your Body (p. 98)

Breathe out three times. Become aware of a pain in your body. Turn your eyes inward and travel down to the location of your pain. See it. What color, what texture, what smell does it have? Breathe out once. Deal with your pain's necessity. (For instance, if it is an inflammation, absorb the red with a piece of white cotton, then throw the piece of cloth over your left shoulder. Breathe out once. Look at the place which is now free of inflammation.)

Visiting Your Body (p. 100)

Visit any part of your body, visiting one of your fingers first. Breathe out once. Turn your eyes inward and travel down to your finger. You are now inside your finger, looking around. What do you sense and see there? Note all the changes and differences between your outer and inner perceptions of your finger. Breathe out once. Open your eyes.

SEVEN

Practicing Life's Quickening Exercises

"A depth of beginning, a depth of end; a depth of good, a depth of evil; a depth of above, a depth of below; a depth of east, a depth of west; a depth of north, a depth of south. The singular Master, God faithful King, dominates them all from His holy dwelling until eternity of eternities."

SEFER YETSIRA, 1:5

If we approach the world of myth objectively, we encounter a huge mass of contradictory, far-fetched stories that severely tax our credulity. Take, for instance, the Greek gods. The mildest thing a rational person can make of them is that they are capricious.

With all the playful irresponsibility of children, one moment they incarnate as all-powerful, beautiful, noble, fair-minded immortals, the next as lying, scheming, jealous, spiteful, revengeful individuals. With dizzying swiftness they appear and disappear, change identities as easily as they would masks, perform in wildly discordant tales, and never excuse or explain themselves, expecting us mere mortals to accept their capering with equanimity.

Take Hecate, the moon goddess. To the ancients, she was known as the hidden one, but she appears also as "Demeter," the radiant goddess of the harvest and mother of all living things (the waxing moon), and as Demeter's golden daughter, the maiden-goddess "Persephone" (the new moon).

When the maiden Persephone is raped and carried away by her Uncle Hades, god of the Underworld and the Dead, (just as Demeter was raped by his brother Zeus, god of the Upper World) Hecate then also becomes "Persephone's shadow," a fitting companion to the Queen of the Dead (the waning moon).

But to the ancients, Hecate was "Artemis" as well, the glowing full moon, a fiercely free, undefiled virgin, and "Medusa" too, one of the three Gorgon sisters. She is the lady whose beautiful face, like the silvery surface of the moon, reflects back to men their unmitigated truth, the vision of which petrifies them. As we have said in chapter 5, one must take precautions with the truth, and Perseus certainly did when he used the mirror of his shield to cut off Medusa's head, making sure not to look at her directly. (When Perseus killed Medusa he was probably Hades, for he wore the cap of invisibility, but it is the name "Perseus" that Hecate incorporates when she is Persephone, "she who was killed by Perseus.")

And perhaps due to the fact that, in vengeance for the loss of Persephone, Hecate, in her attribute as Demeter, goddess of the harvest, causes the whole earth to be barren, she is also known as "Nemesis," goddess of retribution! Moon, mother, daughter, wife? Mother of all *living* things *and* goddess of the *dead*? Radiant, bountiful, grim, implacable, vindictive immortal and also victimized child? Which is she? Who is Hecate *really*?

As emotionally charged as these stories can be, they also have the power to subvert rationality. We will suffer only frustration if we resort to cool reasonableness and employ *only* cool reasonableness in dealing with them. Having come so far, will you suspend judgment here, trusting that you will find the stories' hidden meaning, like a many-facetted jewel, among all their apparent contradictions?

Use the following analogy to help you get your mind around these contradictions. Imagine a red rose in a crystal vase. From where you stand, you can see one side of the flower, its petals very open, some actually beginning to wither at the edges. You also see two leaves, and the beginnings of another, tucked away on the other side of the vase and, in the water, a strong stem with three thorns. Name this side "Demeter."

To see the other side of the rose you will have to turn the vase around or walk around it. Here the petals aren't fully open and you can only see one leaf. Name this side "Persephone."

Do you think that, because you are seeing a second side of the rose, (after having seen its first side), that you have seen the rose in its entirety? I think not! You'd have to check it out from the left ("Medusa"), and the right ("Nemesis"), and look at it from above ("Artemis"), and from below ("Hecate"), to have caught the different angles and perspectives of the rose.

Still, you haven't caught the rose in its immediacy, you haven't caught its *quintessence*. Suddenly a whiff of scent reaches you and for one glorious instant you *experience* rose, you *become* rose, you *are* ROSE! The many faces of the goddess converge in that one instant.

You know her intimately, her various manifestations now combining in her being because, with her scent, you are *living* all of her, as it were, *from the inside*. There *is* no contradiction. It is only when you *step out* that the contradictions appear.

As true disciples of the scientific side of the Enlightenment, we have been taught, and we teach our children, to *step out* and, unfortunately, *to stay out*. Objectivity is our credo. We pride ourselves on being able to distinguish, to separate, to study each aspect of a matter.

Try describing all the different features of the rose you have just seen. It is no mean feat; you may still be trying eighty years from now. Of course, in the process, you may become an expert on roses and your meticulous observations will benefit us all, providing perfumes, soaps, medications, waters, colors, botanical classifications, etc., and we will know more about roses than we ever did. But in the process, have you, like an idol worshiper, become overly engrossed in the exacting pleasures of the *particular*? Have you lost the rose?

It is time we remembered that *experience as a way of knowing* is powerful, valid, and equal in importance to our ability to reason and employ logic as means by which to reach the ultimate goal of "knowledge." Can we re-educate ourselves to remember that *experience* is an equally valid pathway to knowledge?

* * *

BEFORE THE TOWER OF BABEL:
ONE LANGUAGE

Once upon a time, after the Great Flood which purged the world of the wicked and idolatrous, "the whole earth was of one language and of common purpose" (Genesis, 11:1). But men were not content to enjoy their peaceful unity. Fearing to lose it, they decided to build a city and a tower with its top in the heavens. "Let us make a *name* for ourselves, lest we be dispersed across the whole earth" (Genesis 11:4).

As soon as "naming" entered the picture, the men and women who were building the tower became confused. They started to babble (*Ba bel* meaning "confusion has come") and their lofty purpose—to reach God directly—was forgotten in a multiplicity of different "namings" and descriptions.

What is this mysterious first language? Is it indeed lost in the mists of time along with the Tower of Babel? Or is it still present and merely obscured in the mists of our collective subconscious?

The emphasis on "naming" as the cause of our ancestors' scattering (these dispersed people were descended from Shem, whose name means exactly that: "name") suggests that this language was radically different from the ones we now use and that, in fact, this language did not use words.

A clue is given when we are told these people were *of common purpose*. What can this common purpose be? Well, what do we all long for? Happiness, of course, and goodness, love, and peace. *Can our original "one language" be a language of the heart?*

CIRCLING IN TO THE WORDLESS LANGUAGE:
POETRY AND MYTH

If you had never seen a rose before, which would come closer to conjuring up the living thing? The *Botanical Encyclopedia*'s description: a flower, "variously colored, often fragrant" of "any of numerous shrubs or vines of the genus, Rosa, usually having prickly stems, and compound leaves."

Or the poet's?

> *Rose, pure contradiction, delight*
> *in being nobody's sleep under so many*
> *eyelids.*
>
> RILKE

The disease of our modern times is our need to dissect, describe, classify, and interpret experience. With too much information at our fingertips, we are reaching the breaking point where *real meaning* gets lost in the mind's deconstructing processes. Should we, therefore, give up all of our descriptive abilities, all of our powers of analysis, all of our acquired sophistication in naming?

Obviously not, but as the old fairy tale reminds us, it is not dissection but Beauty that seduces the Beast. We need an alternative, a rest from the dryness of logic. We, too, like the Beast, become human when touched by Beauty. We, too, experiencing her loveliness, surrender to love.

As the well-known poet and mythologist Robert Bly puts it, the poet's language, with its "head of emotion," its associative images, its leaps, brings us closer to the real thing. "The farther a poem gets from its initial worldly circumstance without breaking the thread, the more content it has." Is the poet toying with danger? Of course he is! Nothing ventured, nothing gained. What if he breaks the thread and, stretching the limits of credulity, lands us in fantasyland?

Return to Rilke's poem and see if it isn't true that a silent but shattering "aha!" of recognition greets you as you plumb its contents. Do you hear it? It is not just the "delight/in being nobody's sleep under so many/eyelids" that is the cause of the "aha!" but something wordless, indefinable, and beyond the poet's images that his words catapult us into. Like the scent of the rose, the poet's images are signposts to some deeper content—call it the *Source* of the rose.

It is the rose's spirit emerging from the Source that we resonate to, like sounding boards, with an intensity which—dare we say it?— "in-forms" us wholly. Can we, from that *experience*, then go backward and deduce specific characteristics of the rose?

Hecate, our envoy from the mythical realm, allows us to do just that. As she emerges from the numinous depths of experience, her spirit generates fecundity in an unfolding language of images reminiscent of those used by the poet—but they are different, backward.

Hecate does not, like the poet, leap *toward* the Source. Instead, she *rises from it* and, like a many-faceted jewel, she discloses to us—through her different attributes embedded in the stories and images—the movements and patterns of her unfolding spirit manifesting itself in the world.

Compare what she expresses with the language of a physical organism, for example, the cell at conception. The meeting of egg and sperm is the shock, the spark, the experience, that sets the process unfolding. Imagine kicking a box, and seeing all of its secrets come tumbling out. It is as if, at the shock of conception, the first cell turns inside out, to reveal its inner essence unfolding in a patterned movement: the cell splits into two, then four, then groups of four, replicating over and over again.

This secret of life we often see abridged, for instance, in Ezekiel's vision and in many of the mystical texts of the kabbalists and, for those who can read it—revealed—on the tympanums of the great cathedrals. Christ, the seed or first cell, is flanked by the four beasts of Ezekiel's vision—the bull, the lion, the eagle, the man—representing the four human types: the lymphatic, the sanguine, the bilious, and the nervous— four in one. Just as Christ and his four symbolic companion beasts prefigure for us the organic language of our physical selves, the myth of Hecate vividly displays the organic language of the emotional feminine in all of us.

It is all there for us to read—in the myths of the Greek gods, in fairy tales, in the sacred texts of every religion, in ritual ceremonies, in religious iconography. Their patterns and movements, their colors and stories are, in condensed form, the specificities we intensely seek so that we can pinpoint our observations and name them.

As the secrets tumble out of the box—giving us a map of the land, its topography, an itinerary, the dangers—we have another opportunity to catch the tail of the beast and journey back to the Source.

READING THE SACRED LANGUAGE

How do we learn to read the sacred signs that lead us back to the Source? Remember the story of the four rabbis who entered paradise? How did they do it? If we treat this parable from the Midrash (early Jewish oral teachings on the Bible) as a coded text we find that the word "paradise" (*pardes* in Hebrew means "garden") gives us a key to the code.

To enter the Garden, the rabbinical commentators tell us, the four rabbis had to go through four letters, PRDS (*pardes* is written "PRDS" in Hebrew, a language in which vowels do not exist as written letters), and these four letters represent four levels of interpretation of a text.

The first level, P for *pshat*, represents the *literal meaning* of the story or myth. Here we can follow the *logic* of the narration. Each sentence leads to another in a sequence that is self-explanatory. At this level all we care about is that the text be clear and simple:

> "One day as Persephone ran about in the meadow gathering flowers, she strayed away from her mother and the attending nymphs. Suddenly, the ground split open and up from the yawning crevice came a dark chariot drawn by black horses. At the reins stood grim Hades. He seized the terrified girl, turned his horses and plunged back into the ground." *(D'Aulaire's Book of Greek Myths)*

The story has a narrative logic and movement that both fascinates us and gives us our first clue to the way back to the Source. To find the deeper content of the story, simply follow its narrative lead.

The second level, R for *remez*, represents the *allegorical* or *structural level* of the story. Here we notice the subtext: the patterns, similarities, parallelisms, clusters of images, mirror images, reversings, and movements within the story. We only see these when we step back from the story line or, rising above it, consider it—as it were—from the vantage point of the stars. From there, like gods, we can draw a weather map of the story; the streets, spins, spirals, and arrows of its vortex that ultimately throw us into the heart of it.

For instance, with the fall of Hecate from Heaven and Persephone into the Underworld, we notice similarities: both mother and daughter are raped. And patterns emerge: the seed in Persephone's mouth, (she ate a pomegranate seed in the Underworld, which was the reason she must always return there) is similar to Hecate being in the cave. Both images have the same womb-like structure and oval-shaped theme: the cave is oval, as is the seed.

Clusters of images abound: moon, mother, daughter, and it is through an understanding of the flow and the interaction of these patterns that we begin to get an idea of the laws that govern the movements of the imagination. As we learn these laws, we can become an active participant giving creative direction and impetus to our movement back to the Source.

The third level, D for *drash*, is often translated as *interpretation*. *Drash* actually means "to ask." Asking implies a lack. Some missing link, some elusive connection, calls for a question. For instance, why do both Hecate and Persephone fall?

If you give a standard waking answer to that question, finding it in your mind or an outside source, you will end up with what we call an "interpretation." But forget about interpretation, we don't need it here. *Drash* gives us what we need when it offers up its question and, in order to have the question answered properly, we must temporarily leave it alone and suspended over the void, like the bait on a hook at the end of a long fishing line.

The fourth level, S for *sod*, is of course the secret meaning, or *Source*. When shocked, stimulated, or otherwise excited, it turns over and jumps up—a slippery shimmering fish—*to bite the bait*! It comes in response to our question. Its appearance, generated by the power of the question to stimulate the void, creates a new myth.

With these levels in mind, let's briefly go over our "re-imagining" of Persephone's story. The story (P) is but the narrative story, the impetus (R) occurs when the earth opens up and the dreamer finds himself, like Persephone, at the edge of a gaping hole. His questioning self then topples him into the gaping hole (D) where, touching bottom, he shocks the Source into activity (S), firing the imagination to respond.

Thus, like Persephone, or like Rabbi Akiba, (the only one of the four rabbis to successfully go in and come out of the Garden), when the dreamer reemerges, having experienced a radically different configuration (D), he comes out an enhanced and altered person (S).

Can we, like Rabbi Akiba, successfully practice going in and coming out? Instead of being *controlled* by the story lines of our lives—waiting passively for the joys, the blows, and the lessons to present themselves to us—can we look ahead, and pro-actively prepare and educate ourselves to take on more and more of the task beforehand? Can we accelerate the process of enhancement and transformation?

And if so, how, practically, do we *activate* the Source and, firing our reborn imagination into life, begin to rediscover the nature of the elusive, original, one language of the heart? *How do we consciously tap into the Source?*

* * *

PRACTICING THE PLUNGE

The practice I am about to describe has been developed within a long family lineage whose most celebrated exponent and probable originator is the thirteenth-century Provençal kabbalist, Isaac the Blind. In our own time, his direct descendant, Colette Aboulker-Muscat, equaled her predecessors as an innovator, revolutionizing the work that they initiated by her own considerable and unique contributions.

In particular, she brilliantly adapted the work's time-honored methods to modern needs and to people of all creeds and beliefs. While its roots remain essentially Jewish, Sephardic, and Mediterranean, the work employs laws familiar to followers of *all* sacred traditions, essentially because these laws are universal to the *imaginal* mind. We will be describing them as they come up to help you understand the "science" that goes into constructing the "Guided Exercises" you will be using.

To be effective, these Guided Exercises must deploy one or more of the laws inherent in the four levels of PRDS. It is important to understand exactly how *precise* these laws are. As you may know, the custom of guiding individuals or groups of people to form mental visual images is widely practiced; it has even been the subject of serious medical research.

However, visualization is still too often presented with little or no sense of its real power in terms of what it can ultimately achieve. Too often, the exercises people perform remain at the basic *pshat* level which, as we have said, represents the most literal, surface level of the thing.

For centuries the Jesuits, one of the most influential religious orders in Christendom, were trained at the *pshat* level in the imitation of Jesus Christ through the practice of the *Spiritual Exercises* of the order's founder, Saint Ignatius of Loyola. And while I have nothing against the *pshat* level, other laws must be activated to fully exercise one's creative imagination.

To get you going, a slight jolt or shock is necessary. Unless you feel inner tension, you cannot tap the immediacy of the Source and your visualization will lead nowhere. You may have had a pleasant experience but you will have had no experience of *transformation*.

The inner tension I am describing here serves to immerse you completely in the *sensual* experience of the exercise. Having experienced, at one time or another in your life, the feelings of love or grief, you can bear witness to the fact that, when active in you, those feelings engage your *whole* self.

When you are properly jolted by the words of an exercise into experiencing *more* of life, your *whole* self should likewise be engaged. By *embodying* the exercise, you alter your relationship to yourself and to the world. Thus we can say that when you are fully practicing the Guided Exercises, you are practicing a *body* language.

A comparison with the way Yoga postures are performed will give a good picture of what I mean. The Yoga student must consciously form a visual image of a posture—say pushing down with his feet to elongate his spine—at the same time that he *senses* his body assuming the posture. In exactly the same way, the student of the Guided Exercise *senses*, with his *body*, what is happening as he turns the words of the exercise into powerful and constructive imagery.

In fact, the only language your body truly understands and responds to *is* imagery. Therefore, the laws that govern any bodywork like Yoga are the same as those that govern working with mental images. You need not wait for life's difficulties to prod you into activity, but rather, like a good athlete, you can practice being in a state of motion in order to improve your agility to adapt to or transform any given circumstance. When you practice the Guided Exercises, you are purposely setting your different bodies (physical, emotional, mental, spiritual) in motion.

Guided Exercises take no longer than a minute each to practice, unlike the exercises in chapter 5. But, like those exercises, these also find their fulfillment in the dramatic way they help us deal with the problems of daily life. Just as Reversing and practicing the exercise of the Exam of Conscience Backward bring our freedom to choose back to us in situations where imprisoning habits used to rule, so the Guided Exercises free us to calmly face change when it is demanded of us, no matter how drastic it may be.

Having practiced tapping into our Source, we move with agility and are at home with an experience that we very likely used to resist almost automatically. Now we can awaken and strengthen our experience of alignment, just as the Yoga student, pushing down with his feet, practices his posture to coax the body into re-membering alignment.

When life's difficulties throw us off balance, having practiced the exercises, we are intimately "in the know" about alignment and thus are able to fluidly and quickly readjust. We ground our feet, elongate our spines and, without losing a beat, calmly reclaim our balance.

Before we get to the Guided Exercises themselves, let me briefly mention a few important things you need to know upon starting them. In undertaking them, you should choose a quiet time and place. Sit in an armchair, arms relaxed on the armrests and legs uncrossed. Read the exercise to yourself, then closing your eyes, breathe out three times slowly, counting from three to one, seeing the numbers in your mind's eye. See the number one as being tall, clear, and very straight. Now proceed to "sense, see, feel, live" the exercise. Do not "think" about the actual words of the exercise, instead try to experience them imaginally with all your senses.

You should be rewarded with a 3D Technicolor response. When you have completed the exercise, breathe out once and open your eyes. Remember that the Guided Exercises may appear trite when you simply read them or mentally deconstruct them. *Experiencing* them is another matter altogether.

When you are truly present in the exercise, not only your mind, but your whole *being*, is engaged in the process. As we said earlier, the exercise is designed to jolt you into movement, just as a true poem is structured to jolt you with its orchestration of words. Being able to *cause* that jolt, of course, is the challenge, and the art with which the exercise is devised is the answer to that challenge. Using the laws effectively is what makes this happen. I call this the *strategy* of the exercise.

Since you are working from a book, I have chosen simple exercises you can safely do on your own. If for any reason you feel disturbed by what you experience, don't hesitate to seek help. All responses are potentially explosive since the exercises were designed to uncover the true you.

Chapter 3 gives you some help on how to confront and deal with nightmares and difficult dream images. It is no different here. Respond to the necessity of what appears for you and, more importantly, remember to *play!*

I will not list all the laws governing the exercises, but will stick to just those few we have already encountered in our reading of the myth of Persephone earlier in this chapter. You will see how each law governs the set of exercises grouped under it. And although they are grouped to illustrate each law, as much as possible all four levels apply to *all* of the exercises in this chapter.

THE FIRST LAW

Within *pshat,* the story line, is inscribed the *law of imitation.* Are you surprised? Imitation is our first concentrated activity. As infants we learn all we know from imitating our parents and siblings. Later we also learn from the stories we are told. We imitate through imagining ourselves in such roles as the prince killing the dragon, or as Beauty loving the Beast. We experience the Beast's fear, courage, and triumph, or Beauty's budding love and compassion as our own. From this we learn.

This natural and necessary impulse probably never completely stops. Without some kind of role model, positive or negative, to emulate—teacher, star, mentor, hero, saint, or god—what is there to strive for? We use the ability of the imagination to break boundaries and merge, to immerse ourselves in the reality of the person we admire.

There are two ways of putting this law of imitation into effect: we follow the lead of the story line or, we simply *become* the other. Remember, in the imaginal field, your gender, race, and creed do not count. Imagination being fluid, (and democratic) you can easily picture yourself as a man, woman, beast, plant, rock, air, angel, etc. . . .

The tale of *Beauty and the Beast* provides us with a story line we can use here. As the tale begins, Beauty's father loses the family fortune, then hears that one of his ships has survived and is soon to arrive in port. Before he leaves their country house to investigate this rumor, he asks his three daughters what gifts they would like him to purchase for them with the proceeds from the ship's cargo.

The two elder daughters both ask for expensive jewels and dresses, while Beauty, quite rightly concerned that the money might *not* arrive, says that since there are no roses at their new home and she misses them greatly, she wants nothing but a single rose.

Later, her father, poorer than when he set out, gets lost in the woods on his way home. Looking for a way out of the woods, he finds instead the Beast's deserted magic castle and its beautiful gardens. It is the single rose that he doesn't hesitate to pick from those gardens that immediately brings the Beast out of hiding in a horrible rage.

Monster that he is, the Beast demands possession of one of the man's daughters to make amends for his theft of the rose. As good as she is beautiful, Beauty is the only one of the three daughters who is willing to make the sacrifice of leaving the familiar safety of her father's home to go and live with the very strange and terrifying Beast.

Guided Exercise 1 (Imitation I)

Breathe out three times. Imagine that, like Beauty, you must leave your home and the protection of those who love you. What are you sensing and feeling?

Guided Exercise 2 (Imitation II)

Breathe out once. See yourself as Beauty walking for the first time in the Beast's strange garden. You discover his rose bush. Breathe out once. What do you feel and see when you smell the one perfect rose on the rose bush?

THE SECOND SET OF LAWS

Within *remez*, the structure, are hidden the *laws of movement,* of which there are many. We begin with those that come under the heading of *directionality*. In the story of *Beauty and the Beast*, the father takes a wrong direction, whereupon his life, his daughter's, and the Beast's, are changed forever. Going up or down, left or right, backward or forward, produce different outcomes. Can we specify them?

Exploring all six directions allows a dreamer not only to exercise these possibilities but to discover their attributes. Suppose you are faced with a complex situation at home. Exploring all six directions may help you uncover the various dynamics that are at play for you.

Guided Exercise 3 (Directionality)

Breathe out once. Sense, see, feel like Beauty, returning back to your father's house after having been absent for a very long time. Which direction do you take to go home? (Right, left, straight, forward, back, up, down) Breathe out once. What do you see when you first arrive? What are your feelings?

Guided Exercise 4 (Penetration I)

Breathe out once. Imagine yourself as Beauty looking down into the center of the rose. Can you smell it? Breathe out once. What do you see there? What happens?

What are the attributes of each direction? Pushing the levels of *penetration* can make these clearer. Pushing forward, opening the next door, and the next, may eventually allow you to see and experience something new. (For instance, you could open another door at the end of another corridor and emerge in the sunlight in a beautiful garden.) Pushing further and further along a chosen direction is a strategy for movement. Think how useful this strategy may be for someone confronted with a knotty situation that doesn't appear to have an answer.

Guided Exercise 5 (Penetration II)

Breathe out once. Imagine that you are standing in front of a locked door. You are holding a key chain full of keys. Find the key that fits the lock. Insert it into the lock, turn the key and open the door. What do you see? What do you do? Breathe out once. Do you stand at the threshold or do you walk through?

If the strategy of penetration—pushing forward in one direction—doesn't break the pattern, what do you do? Directions work in pairs. "Down" works with "up" (after Persephone's fall, she rises again) and "right" works with "left."

Many of us favor one direction over the other. Suppose you are obsessively building your future and have no time to reflect or look back upon your life. The direction you then favor is the right. (The future translates as the right in the imaginal field.) Or, you are always looking to ascend *out* of your body, into your mental or fantasy worlds. Having found that this way of escaping your pains and responsibilities is more natural for you, the direction you favor is up.

Both are survival techniques, probably acquired in childhood, and may no longer serve you. Continually exploring one direction to the exclusion of the others is an impoverishment. To become true dreamers we need to explore *all* directions.

Suppose someone is constantly harping back to their past, this translates as the left in the imaginal field. Thus, doing an exercise that takes that person to the right, the future, may create a movement strong enough to jolt them from their obsession with the past. (Stimulated by the jolt, that person's imagination unfolds an unexpected, new configuration that impresses them to the point of weakening or actually wiping away their obsessive stranglehold on their images of the past.)

Reinstating fluid movement in the left-right imaginal axis revitalizes one's ability to move in *all* directions. This basic strategy for change means turning around, going the other way. (This concept we have previously discussed as Tshuva, repentance in Hebrew.) Let's identify this turn-around, or this switch, to the other pole of the pair, as the *law of return*. Return helps to break repetition in that it allows the opposite point of view to be experienced.

Guided Exercise 6 (Return)

Breathe out three times. Visualize someone with whom you are currently having some difficulty. Imagine yourself stepping out of your body, walking over to that person, and entering into his or her body. How does it feel inside this body? Is it spacious or tight? Dark or light? Calm or agitated? How does this person breathe, move, think? Breathe out once. From this new vantage point within this body and brain, look back at yourself. How do you, through that person's eyes, see yourself? What do you sense and feel? What do you say to the "you" standing opposite? Say it, and hear it, in this person's voice. Breathe out once. Returning to your own body, look back at the person you just visited. Have your perception and feelings about that person changed? If so, describe the change to yourself.

This exercise is similar to the exercise on pages 88–89, where it is part of the Exam of Conscience Backward. But here, instead of just stepping into the other person's shoes, you have visited another's body. You should find the effect of "repentance" stronger.

Guided Exercise 7 (Pairing)

Breathe out three times. See and sense yourself as a fully grown tree. Sense and see your roots, trunk, branches, and leaves. Breathe out once. Now sense and see the leaves telescoping very quickly back into the branches, the branches into the trunk, into the roots, into the seed. Breathe out once. Sense and see yourself as the seed. Hear the murmur of your own life. What is it saying? Breathe out once. Now growing very quickly, return to being a fully grown tree.

Pairing naturally leads us to consider *mirroring* as another law of movement. Mirroring adds a further twist to the law of return. The mirror reflects back to us our image reversed. In other words, the image is turned around. The effect is to let us see—to return to us—what we couldn't or wouldn't see otherwise.

Being unaccustomed to this other point of view, we are jolted into movement. Whether we feel shock, surprise, pleasure, or sorrow, none of us remain indifferent to our own image. If you feel uncomfortable about yourself and want to know why, looking into the mirror will enlighten you. Isn't this the first step toward correcting yourself?

Mirroring doesn't only imply looking into a physical or imaginal mirror. A reversed image is projected back to us whenever we are engaged in the *act* of looking. That is the way our eyes work. When we are looking into the imaginal world or when we are dreaming at night, the dream images return to us our inner being, just as a video taken of you will return to you your image of yourself walking and talking, something you cannot see otherwise.

There is a centrifugal movement in looking, which attracts a centripetal response. For instance, suppose someone is obsessed with making money and getting ahead, to the point of forgetting what is right or wrong. His dream images (the reverse pairing of the day vision) will reflect back to him those forgotten parts, often in a "resentful" nightmarish way. ("How can you forget us?" the dream images seem to ask.)

This same law happens, not only in night dream, but *whenever* we look within. When we do our exercises the simple fact that we are looking within means that the imaginal response we get will be reversed. Therein lies its surprise and effectiveness. The same law applies to everyday life.

This brings to mind my friend who always carried a gun on the subway. Why? "Because," said he, "there are so many angry people out there." What if he were to give up his gun? Would he encounter as many angry people? His fear—symbolized by his carrying of the gun—creates the centripetal response: fear gravitates toward anger.

Using the mirroring strategy will help us understand how we are fabricating our own reality, while at the same time it will allow us to see what changes we need to initiate.

 ### Guided Exercise 8 (Mirroring)

Breathe out three times. Imagine looking into a mirror at yourself. How do you see yourself? What are you wearing? What expression do you have? How do you feel upon seeing yourself in the mirror?

Mirroring leads us to contemplate the possible juxtaposition of two completely opposing images, for instance Beauty and the Beast, as a "shocking" contrast. This is the *law of opposites*. The "shock" enables the blocked movement present in dichotomies (such as either-or, good and evil, beauty and beastliness) to "explode" into a new but fluid configuration. In other words, a new insight has occurred and the dreaming is restored.

 ### Guided Exercise 9 (Opposites)

Breathe out once. Imagine being, at the same time, Beauty and the Beast. What happens? What do you feel?

Paying attention to clusters of images is another way of measuring the depths. For instance Hecate, Persephone, and Demeter are one and the same, says the myth. We are being told something, but what?

Suppose that in your daily life a situation arises wherein three different ideas tug at you and will not let go. Why are they there? They seem not to belong together, nevertheless they pop up in your mind again and again around the same situation or issue. What do you do?

When we allow the imaginal mind to hold different tendencies, directions, and possibilities together simultaneously, a new movement explodes out of their tension. Thus the flow is reestablished. This is called the *law of clustering*.

Guided Exercise 10 (Clustering)

Breathe out once. See Hecate the feminine spirit, Persephone the maiden, and Demeter the mother, as the three points of a triangle. Breathe out once. Look into the center of the triangle. What do you see?

What if you are feeling that you are two people at once? One moment you are sweet and accommodating, the next an out-of-control, angry person. How do you learn to enfold these different aspects of yourself into a totality? How do you resolve the split between the two tendencies?

As I hope the preceding exercises have demonstrated, the dream world allows us to jump from one point to another in a flash. It also allows us to embody different forms at will. Transforming from one to another and allowing ourselves to experience different alternatives gives us the agility to be flexible and to change rapidly and gracefully. Remember, these Guided Exercises are transformational. Here you can actually use the *malleability* of your imagination to practice not only movement, but instantaneous transformation.

Guided Exercise 11 (Malleability I)

Breathe out once. See the beastly side of yourself. Breathe out once. Imagine being Beauty caressing your beastly side. What happens?

Guided Exercise 12 (Malleability II)

Breathe out once. Imagine entering into a garden where there are many animals. Imagine entering into the body of a lizard; breathe out once; of a peacock; breathe out once; of a bird.

THE THIRD LAW: OPEN-ENDEDNESS

Within the level of *drash*, (the question), is inscribed the *law of open-endedness*. If we set out to ask a question and rush to answer it, we haven't allowed the question to hang suspended over the void. We haven't *listened*.

Open-endedness creates the space for a response to come. Let's call this space a "pause." The pause is not only the secret of knowing yourself, it is the secret of all healing. Within the pause, the response finds room to emerge. Open-endedness allows the source to be triggered and the imagination to unfold creatively. (Open-endedness is different than another type of situation which occurs when a "leading question" is offered up. A leading question, unlike the results which occur when the law of open-endedness is put into play, will inevitably draw the dreamer to a *foregone* conclusion. In only one case is this acceptable and even advisable. That is when the exercise is meant to heal a specific physical condition, and is known to provoke the desired response.)

THE FOURTH LAW: IMMEDIACY

Within *sod*, the fourth level, the level of the Source, the *law of immediacy* is inscribed. Remember how the source *jumps* to the question. All of the Guided Exercises must be short. As we have seen earlier in this chapter, tapping into the source requires surprise tactics. Blurring the surprise by lengthening the process undercuts the necessary spontaneity and freshness of the process. The response must be quick; its unfolding doesn't require more than a minute. Remember that tapping into the source means tapping into the heart of the matter, into feeling.

The imaginal response is holographic, existing as it does in the language of dreaming. The first image contains *all* of the truth. If you linger because you don't like the image, you may be tempted to exchange it for another you like better. But how will you ever learn to focus your imagination if, at the very beginning, you are already questioning its validity?

Remember also that lingering incites fantasizing. Believe in what you see the first instant, however unpleasant or strange you may deem it to be. Immediacy is a strategy for transformation. It is the only way to become a true dreamer.

 ### Guided Exercise 13 (Immediacy)

Breathe out once. Imagine that, with a magnifying glass, you look at a word written on an ancient papyrus you just discovered. What do you read?

I have just shown you some of the basic strategies for inducing movement in a dreamer. Using the Guided Exercises as practice for inner development is what I propose to you. (See appendix 1 for another example of a series of exercises.) Unless otherwise indicated, doing them once is enough. If you want to do them again, wait an interval of at least three months so as to conserve the effect of surprise.

* * *

You are now ready to move on to your eighth task: exploring the fundamental intention of your being. Before moving on, however, make sure that you are familiar and comfortable with all your previous tasks. Without them you cannot proceed. They are the basis for the second half of the work—becoming a focused dreamer and Master of the Life Plan.

A QUICK REFERENCE GUIDE TO CHAPTER 7 EXERCISES

Imitation I (p. 114)

Breathe out three times. Imagine that, like Beauty from the tale of Beauty and the Beast, you must leave your home and the protection of those who love you. What are you sensing and feeling?

Imitation II (p. 114)

Breathe out once. See yourself as Beauty walking for the first time in the Beast's strange garden. You discover his rose bush. Breathe out once. What do you feel and see when you smell the one perfect rose on the rose bush?

Directionality (p. 114)

Breathe out once. Sense, see, feel like Beauty, returning back to your father's house after having been absent for a very long time. Which direction do you take to go home? (Right, left, straight, forward, back, up, down?) Breathe out once. What do you see when you first arrive at your father's house? What are your feelings?

Penetration I (p. 115)

Breathe out once. Imagine yourself as Beauty looking down into the center of the rose. Can you smell it? Breathe out once. What do you see there? What happens?

Penetration II (p. 115)

Breathe out once. Imagine that you are standing in front of a locked door. You are holding a key chain full of keys. Find the key that fits the lock. Insert it into the lock, then turn the key and open the door. What do you see? What do you do? Breathe out once. Do you stand at the threshold or do you walk through the door?

Return (p. 116)

Breathe out three times. Visualize someone with whom you are currently having some difficulty. Imagine yourself stepping out of your body, walking over to that person, and entering their body. How does it feel inside that person's body? Is it spacious or tight? Dark or light? Calm or agitated? How does this person breathe, move, and think? Breathe out once. From this new vantage point within their body and brain, look back at yourself. How do you, through that person's eyes, see yourself? What do you sense and feel? What do you say to the "you" standing opposite? Say it, and hear it, in that person's voice. Breathe out once. Returning to your own body, look back at the person you just visited. Have your perceptions and feelings about that person changed? If so, please describe the change to yourself.

Pairing (p. 117)

Breathe out three times. See and sense yourself as a fully grown tree. Sense and see your roots, trunk, branches, and leaves. Breathe out once. Now sense and see the leaves telescoping very quickly back into the branches, the branches into the trunk, into the roots, and into the seed. Breathe out once. Sense and see yourself as that seed. Hear the murmur of your own life. What is it saying? Breathe out once. Now, growing very quickly, return to being a full-grown tree.

Mirroring (p. 118)

Breathe out three times. Imagine looking into a mirror at yourself. How do you see yourself? What are you wearing? What expression do you have on your face? How do you feel upon seeing yourself in the mirror?

Opposites (p. 118)

Breathe out once. Imagine being, at the same time, Beauty and the Beast. What happens? What do you feel?

Clustering (p. 119)

Breathe out once. See Hecate the feminine spirit, Persephone the maiden, and Demeter the mother, as three points of a triangle. Breathe out once. Look into the center of the triangle. What do you see?

Malleability I (p. 119)

Breathe out once. See the beastly side of yourself. Breathe out once again. Imagine being Beauty caressing your beastly side. What happens?

Malleability II (p. 120)

Breathe out once. Imagine entering into a garden where there are many animals. Imagine entering into the body of a lizard, breathe out once. Imagine entering into the body of a peacock, breathe out once. Imagine entering into the body of a bird.

Immediacy (p. 121)

Breathe out once. Imagine that, with a magnifying glass, you look at a word written on an ancient papyrus you have just discovered. What do you read?

Go to appendix 1 for another example of a series of exercises. Do them all in one sitting. (p. 202)

EIGHT

Intent and Dreaming

"The vision that he sees is far ahead, and he prophesies for the distant future."

EZEKIEL 12:27

Once upon a time, in the holy city of Jerusalem, where miracles happen as naturally as a butterfly lands on blossoms, there lived a young Arab boy, maybe fourteen years old. Nabulsi was his name. He had no family or home. All his earthly possessions were on his back and in his pocket was a coin to pay for his dinner. He was not the only lost soul wandering through the Old City bazaar—there were many like him— but this day, unbeknownst to him, the Spirit hovered.

Nabulsi's eye caught a glint of sunlight on an object that was propped, among other spoils, on a carpet in the street. He stopped to look. It was a doorknocker.

Suddenly, he had a vision of the doorknocker hanging on a door! Behind the door appeared a house, and behind the house, as if in transparency, another knocker on another door and another house, then another knocker, door, and house, and so on as far as the boy's gaze could reach. The doorknocker was beautiful and he loved it, but his vision caught his breath. There is nothing like a vision to knock all "conventional" sense out of you. He bought the doorknocker with the coin that was supposed to pay for his dinner.

It had started with a vision of many doors and many houses, and continued with an action: Nabulsi bought the knocker. Crazy, or courageous? That night the boy went hungry, huddled against the cold

125

on a dark street corner, hugging a heavy doorknocker to his narrow chest. Is that the end of his story? Or, through the fusion of vision and action, was a movement set off that would not abate until coming full circle, until the dream propelled itself into reality?

Is "vision" a prophetic message from the gods? Or a blueprint of our inner structure that, when unfolded, reveals the true purpose of our being? Either way, will Nabulsi grapple with its promise and pursue the destiny it foretells? And, if so, what is the power of this vision that it can so grab hold of a man (or woman) as to drive him (or her), against all odds, to make his (or her) dream come true?

We may not all be blessed with a vision as potent as this boy had. As it turned out, he was illumined by the Spirit and he ran with it. If we don't have the same kind of clear vision does it mean we are missing our blueprint? Or simply that our higher purpose remains hidden? Or have we been offered a vision but ignored or rejected it, preferring distractions to the single-pointed focus of pursuing a dream? Can we hope that, in time, we will have a vision of our true purpose in life and that that vision will be strong enough to thrust us into action?

* * *

INTENT STARTS WITH A VISION

"In the beginning God created the heavens and the earth" (Genesis 1:1). From what did He create them and all the wonders that they contain? "Creatio ex nihilo": nothingness? "No," says the Midrash. God looked and saw "letters written in black fire upon white fire." But there was no fire before the world was created!

What fire can this be if not the burning exaltation of God seeing Himself? All that He contained, His dreaming of Himself, fired up creation. He saw that "It was very good" (Genesis 1:31), and His passion for what He saw was the fuel that brought the world into manifestation. That élan He gifted to us and, with it (since we are made in His image) He gifted us with the know-how to become manifestors and co-creators in His plan. But *co-creators with God*? What kind of magical thinking is this? What dangerous folly?

A voice is saying, "Look within and the fire of thy looking will propel thy dreaming into manifestation." This is fine, except that the vigilant mother says to her child, "Don't dream your life away. Dreaming leads nowhere." So who is right? Well, both, of course. Let us see why.

In the beginning, *bereshit*, is the seed. Having neither past nor future, it is the instant, the shock of revelation. Unpacking the seed takes six days (six dreaming movements?) and, on the seventh day, the seed rests in its glorious unfolding, a Tree of Life. But still there is no manifestation. Manifestation will take place in the second phase of creation when the order is reversed. This is when God makes "earth and heaven" (Genesis 2:4) as opposed to "heaven and earth" (Genesis 1:1).

It is in Genesis 2:7 that God takes earth and fashions Adam. His practical—or should we say "down-to-earth"?—gesture brings His dream into physical manifestation just as, more humbly, Nabulsi's gesture of buying the knocker brings *his* dream into reality.

Is this enough? Well, no! The world of manifestation exists in time and space. Buying the knocker or fashioning Adam is not the whole story. Since the dream is due to manifest in the physical world, the existence of time and space impose their own unfolding needs and necessities upon the situation. After God made Adam, God saw further that, "It is not good that man be alone; I will make him a helper corresponding to him" (Genesis 2:18). So He fashioned Eve and brought her to Adam.

Following in this same way of physical necessity, Nabulsi, having committed himself to the doorknocker, is now fired up with the necessity of finding a place to store his treasure until the day comes when he can buy the house that will frame the door on which he can hang his precious doorknocker. His passion to find good work that will advance his prospects in life is fuelled by his vision. He is no longer a hopeless boy, but a new man, one with a purpose—his intent, or *kavanah* as the Hebrews call it—burning in his heart and mind and body.

Each step of the way, because we live in a limiting physical reality, Nabulsi's kavanah will be challenged. What if he were offered a well-paying job, with room and board, as a shepherd in Galilee? He'd be far from the city, where he knows his dream has squarely placed him. Will he allow his immediate needs and desires to pull him away from the pursuit of his vision, from what he knows intimately in his gut is his one true purpose in life?

It is how he chooses but, more importantly, how he *acts* upon his choices that will determine whether he lives a life driven by expediency and willfulness or a life full of purpose and meaning. His vision was an annunciation. Now it must be submitted to; it must be lived.

THE DIFFERENCE BETWEEN
KAVANAH AND WILL

What if the boy had not seized upon the opportunity? What if, out of fear, he had refused the necessity of the revelation? What if he had not bought the doorknocker? Then he would be like the servant in Christ's parable of the talents who takes the three coins his master gives him and buries them in the garden for safekeeping. The coins won't fructify.

But still, the vision of what could have been haunts him, like a soul without roots. At this point the vigilant mother is justified in saying: "Don't dream your life away!" For if you do not work hard to turn your dream into a physical reality, it will revert to being a fantasy, a stagnant play of your imagination, a guilt, a regret.

What goals can the mother propose in place of her child's? Financial security, social standing, marital happiness, popularity, becoming a doctor, a lawyer, or a star, as she herself had dreamed of becoming. Those goals seem perfectly justified—but for one fact. They are someone else's. They are fuelled by the mother's own dreams, desires, and fears. The child may aspire to them too, because he/she is ambitious, competitive, envious, easily swayed, or because the child simply wants to assuage the mother's needs. They are arrived at *from the outside*, by a mental process of either elimination or calculation.

Because these "busy dreams" (that we and our loved ones can be very industrious in promoting) originate in the sticky realm of emotions and reactions, the pure fire we have called kavanah is not there to propel them. Instead, a lesser sort of fire, not the all-consuming, pure flame of purpose, but of a wasting kind, takes hold of us. We are driven to control the environment, or impose our will, or grab the chosen goal before it can be held, or we collapse into impotence and despair.

Either way, the process has little grace for us, it is not fluid and easy.

Since the energy at our disposal is being "re-active," (see the Life Plan chart, figure 5), we can only use *force* to break down any opposition that stands in the way of our calculated goal.

What is so bad about that? Better to be willful than apathetic, successful than not. Yet how many successful people who, in *our* eyes possess all we ever dreamed of having, take drugs or commit suicide because, in *their* eyes, their life is a failure or simply meaningless? How else can one explain their despair? It is plain that their dreams have been false dreams, fuelled, as we have seen, by anger, ambition, resentment, envy, cowardice; emotions that, like the Furies of Greek mythology, pursue us to drive us crazy.

Imagine that you are a football player, you have the ball and are angrily charging through your opponents' ranks to make a touchdown. Everyone is cheering as you cross the goal line, you feel justified and pumped up with pride! You have just used your will to break through fierce resistance, and you have been successful.

Now imagine a different scenario: you have just caught the ball and, in that split second, it just happens! Like it "just happened" to Nabulsi, you plunge into the Source, you "see" yourself effortlessly making the touchdown. As if by magic, the cheering recedes like a great wave into silence, the stadium is oh-so-remote, the opposing team and you, together with all your teammates, are moving in slow motion. You are especially struck by the ease and fluidity of your gestures.

It all happens as if eternity is yours, yet in the instant of "seeing" yourself make the touchdown, you are already *at* the touchdown, just as in the dream time. Sports people call this phenomenon "the Zone." Athletes who have experienced it never forget their sudden leap into "stardom." They have "seen" divinity in action: the "true" vision transforming their limitations into victory.

True visions arise from our source. Kavanah, fired by true vision, creates the Zone. If you take your intention from your Source and follow kavanah, it all becomes easy, fluid, simple. When it becomes complicated and difficult, your dreaming has gone off track. You are using force to try to make something happen that is not meant to be. Using your will this way can be very exhausting.

THE RAINBOW OF FEELINGS

So what then is a true vision? Since Adam and Eve lost the Garden of Eden we know that we must labor and toil to bring out the treasure hidden in our earth. We experience it every day. We make efforts in our job, we rush to take care of our children and elderly parents, we work to hold onto a troubled relationship, we try with all our will, gritting our teeth, to stay afloat in a difficult world.

What else can we do if we haven't been given the gift of a true vision? We are not all as lucky as Nabulsi. Hold on! This is getting complicated. I can already hear your rage: Why him and not me? Why is it easy for him, and for me so hard? Why is he passionate and I am exhausted? Only by finding out what a true vision is will you begin to answer those questions. But first, do we know it exists?

Old tales tell us there is a pot of gold buried at the foot of the rainbow. It is our inheritance if we dare claim it. We can only reach the gold, the alchemical stone, the Source if, having discarded all our "busy" dreams, we dare to walk the seven-fold path of the rainbow.

The Rainbow

Breathe out three times. Imagine that you are climbing the great arc of a rainbow. Jump and play in each of the different colors—red, orange, yellow, green, blue, indigo, violet. Feel how each produces a different sensation in your body and a different feeling. Can you give these feelings names? Breathe out once. Walk all the way to the end of the rainbow to find the treasure buried at the foot of it.

When we step on the earth at the other side of the rainbow we are in the Zone, powered by the Source whose mystery and strength are too great for us to fathom. From its soft, strong light irradiate all the colors of our feelings. Remember, our feelings are not emotions. Emotions are reactions to blocked desires, expectations, claims, etc. Refresh your memory by looking at the Life Plan chart (figure 5). When we *react*, we are still in opposition, pushing against or pulling away, playing the "willful" game (see chapter 2).

But when we *feel* (love, compassion, beauty, strength, splendor, courage, victory, joy, mercy, justice, etc.), we send out light and warmth in all directions, like the pot of gold or the sun in the sky. We glow. In the truest sense of the word, we become stars.

The pot of gold at the foot of the rainbow is an inheritance that is offered not only to the Nabulsis of this world but to us all. Yes! That means you and me and the tinker, the tailor, the rich, the poor, the black, the white. Being all light, the Source knows no distinction. Form has not unfurled from it nor yet been made manifest by our choices. Like Joseph, the Dreamer in the Bible, we are all the favorite son/daughter, and our father—the Spirit that blows the fire of life into us—drapes us in the robe of many colors. (I use the example of Joseph here because the male gender represents the "active" part in us. Joseph in Hebrew means added.)

We will have to discard all the "busy" dreams if we want to reclaim our inheritance: that other son, the vision, that will be "added" to the gift (the Imagination) that we were born with.

ONLY THE GREAT DREAM FUELS INTENT

Joseph was young like Merlin and like the little helpers of the "seeing" world. He was in love with his own beauty, which shouldn't surprise us, the dream world being so enchanting for the dreamer. He had a dream that he told his brothers.

"Behold! We were binding sheaves in the middle of the field when, behold! My sheaf arose and remained standing; then behold! Your sheaves gathered around and bowed down to my sheaf."

How could Joseph fail to recognize the effect his words would have on his brothers? Was he just too vain for his own good or was he simply naive? On the contrary, like all the little helpers of the dream world, Joseph was an innocent. So much so that, wanting to make sure his brothers had indeed heard him, he dreamt another dream with the same pattern, thus "adding" insult to injury.

"Behold! The sun, the moon, and eleven stars were bowing down to me" (Genesis 37:9). Joseph's brothers were understandably incensed and admonished him: "Would you then reign over us? Would you then dominate us?" Joseph's father scolded him, for indeed Joseph had needlessly provoked him and his sons, but Joseph's father, "kept the matter in mind." Why?

Do you recognize the pattern? Joseph is the central hub, while the brothers, father (sun), and mother (moon) are the spokes of the wheel. This is a "feeling" dream! It irradiates a star-like glow, attracting to it all the protagonists. Just as Joseph's father couldn't forget his son's dream, the brothers couldn't forget it either.

Indeed, a dream that glows leaves an indelible impression, not only on the dreamer, but on all who hear it. It burns in our minds, unforgettable. It sets a new vision in motion and keeps it going until such time as the vision completes itself by making manifest—in the physical world—its message. Having come to fruition, it then enters the world of our most cherished memories, or becomes the food of sacred tales, myths, legends, and fairy tales.

When the Source has been tapped and is revealing its fundamental and true construct in the form of a night dream, we call it a "great dream," to distinguish it from the busy dreams. When it appears in the daytime, as it did to the Arab boy, we call it a "prophetic vision."

The great dream (night) or the prophetic vision (day) are the only types of dreaming that create intent. Close to the incandescent Source, where only feeling can flourish and survive, they fuel the movement of kavanah.

TEARS IN THE VISION

It is all very well to have a powerful and sudden vision in the daytime. The event is shocking enough that we may, perhaps, allow ourselves to believe in its authenticity. But a night dream? Obviously Joseph thought his dream was so important he had to tell everyone!

In fact, he had the dream in two different versions. Risking his brothers' anger, he told it twice! Who are the brothers that hate and envy Joseph so? By now, surely you know. They are the other parts, the emotions of reaction in Joseph that resist the vision. They are the movements of our earth, of our natural habitat, the body: our instincts and desires, our violent reactions and confused emotions, our bad habits that don't want to be ousted or moved by kavanah.

These are the culprits that, like animals, tear apart our robe of many colors and, mixing its colors, breed the busy dreams. They don't want us to have anything to do with the great dream. Against such odds as these even a great sage like Joseph nearly succumbed. The brothers tore his robe and threw him into a snake pit, and when that didn't seem enough, they sold him to the Ishmaelites.

How, then, are we to identify and authenticate our great dream?

How do we recognize that we have already been visited? Or that we need to elicit the great dream which lives in us?

What characterizes great dreams? Their classic structure, clear colors, compactness, beauty, impact, simplicity. Great dreams are like good poetry, we trust them. Or like a good lover: strong, sweet, pliant, inciting. Beacons, they illuminate and guide us and we can never forget them.

Yet, like the brothers, we fight to destroy them. But don't you know that they are indestructible? We can bury them, smother them, hack them up, but still they shine forth in the most unexpected moments. If you think you haven't been visited by a great dream, you are probably wrong. The Source in us never ceases to shine.

Here is one way to remember:

First Memory

Breathe out three times. Return backward through your past to your first happy memory. Recall it and live it intensely, in all its magical details and nuances. Breathe out once. Returning forward through your past, recognize how this first memory has fuelled your inspiration and driven your life.

If you do not easily find a first happy memory, then try this exercise:

Facing Your Ultimate Kavanah

Breathe out three times. Imagine that you are seeing yourself at the end of your life. What kind of a human being is standing before you? Look into its eyes and glean there the accomplishments, qualities, and essence it embodies. Breathe out once. Know what has driven this human being to become who he/she is, and recognize this drive as the kavanah you are looking for. If possible give your kavanah a name.

Don't worry whether your first memory is an authentic memory or simply a "screen memory" (a recollection of an event that you were either told about and recall as if it were an authentic memory, or an event that may not even have happened), because either type is capable of becoming your personal myth, as it is its effect on you that is important. Both exercises—reminding yourself of your first strong, happy "memory" or rolling time forward to the place where life ends—will bring you to a renewal with the fundamental purpose of your being. Do both these exercises. Remember that it is the vision, in all its encapsulated intensity and richness, that fuels kavanah.

* * *

But is one single vision always powerful enough to keep us going? Even when we are confident that we have identified a fundamental purpose that, like a bridge of light links all of our actions, we may nonetheless need reminders along the way. We may need more specific guidance.

How do you break down the journey into parts, and, under the umbrella of your fundamental purpose, develop a specific kavanah for each segment of your odyssey? This will be your ninth task.

A QUICK REFERENCE GUIDE TO CHAPTER 8 EXERCISES

The Rainbow: To Reach the Source (p. 130)

Breathe out three times. Climb the rainbow, play in each color, pay attention to the feeling each color evokes in you, and give it a name. Breathe out once. Walk to the end of the rainbow to find the treasure buried at its foot.

First Memory: To Remember a Great Dream (p. 133)

Breathe out three times. Return back to your first happy memory. Breathe out once. Come back through your past, recognizing how this first memory has fuelled your inspiration and driven your life.

Facing Your Ultimate Kavanah (p. 133)

Breathe out three times. See yourself at the end of your life. What kind of a human being is standing before you? Recognize your qualities and know what has driven you to become who you are. See this drive as the kavanah (intent) you are looking for, and give it a name.

NINE

The Waking Dream

"The (Jewish) sages said to Alexander: 'This is the eyeball of a human being. It is never satisfied.'"

TALMUD, TAMID 32B

It is rare that, having found our true purpose in life, our prince or princess of light, we should live happily ever after with never a moment's struggle. That kind of happy ending only happens in fairy tales. And while it may seem sad, it is probably a good thing, since engaging in struggle is the very thing that enables us to stay healthy and to perfect ourselves.

At some point on our journey we will undoubtedly come across a Gordian knot, a seemingly unsolvable problem that, if we remain true to the prompting of our conscious mind, we must try to unravel, dissect, or deconstruct. The intellect, when faced with a problem, goes at it with bared teeth and a take-no-prisoners attitude that usually only manages to make matters worse. The Gordian knot won't unknot, the answer won't come: the writer has writer's block, the lover hesitates to commit, the student vacillates between careers, or an impasse has been reached and there seems no way to get beyond it.

You have learned by now that we have two minds: the logical and the imaginal. If one isn't helping you cut through your impasse, why not try the other?

Have you ever danced the tango? It is a tantalizing give-and-take, full of dagger looks and legs, formality and entwining. The two partners merge and separate, he leads, she captivates. There is a pattern in the fluidly orchestrated repartee of this dance that I hope you are beginning to recognize, since it perfectly models the way our conscious and sub-conscious minds partner each other, engaging, as they do, in a movement that dissolves old patterns to create vital new ways of being. When and how do we begin this dance?

* * *

DEALING WITH AMBIVALENCE

When things are not going as well as we would want them to, we tend to fantasize about other people's successful lives. We envy them the ease of their progress, not realizing that they, too, have gone through their ups and downs. None of us are immune to the inexorable order of things. In the words of the author of Ecclesiastes 3:4, "There is a time to laugh and a time to cry."

The only real difference between you and those you envy is a difference in timing. Like the phoenix, they have resurrected themselves from their ashes, whereas so far you haven't been able to do so. Even when you are in possession of the inestimable treasure of having discovered your purpose in life, you still must face the struggles inherent in *accomplishing* that purpose.

Plus, you can be sure that along the way you will have to deal with life's inevitable vagaries, irrationalities, and injustices. Or the reason you feel that your life is a failure may be that you are simply at loose ends, having reached the end of one stage of your journey but are now unsure of how to proceed.

Despite the fact that Job's name has come to stand for human struggle and suffering, if you read his whole story you will discover that God's purpose for him was to be a happy man, blessed with wisdom, health, wives, children, land, and flocks in abundance.

Did Job's conscious mind help him during his trials? Certainly there was no logic that could wipe away the horror of the deaths of his sons and daughters. Early on Job does say, "I desire to reason with God" (Job 13:3) but, as his sufferings continue, there are no well thought-out arguments that can answer his heart-breaking lamentations.

Our tribulations may not be as epic as Job's, but we all will encounter, in more or less dramatic ways, no-win situations, deadlocks, or wastelands, moments of emptiness, or maybe just mild, unfocused depression from which logic seems unable to extricate us. We are fluent in describing the ins and outs of our situation but incompetent in our ability to resolve it. We hesitate, we tergiversate, we obsess, we wallow in ambivalence.

Our problems turn into Gordian knots ever more complex and unsolvable as we try our logic at unknotting them but cannot find the loose end that would guide us in. We exhaust ourselves hoping to make sense of these knots, only to find ourselves sinking deeper into a morass of indecision. How do we extricate ourselves?

ORACLES AND PARADOX

Let us listen to the story of Alexander the Great and the original Gordian knot. It begins with an old chariot that rested for hundreds of years within the walls of the temple of Zeus Basileus on the acropolis of Gordium, the ancient capital of Phrygia (the key-road junction in central Anatolia). Legend has it that Gordius, father of the mythical king Midas, had migrated from Macedonia in this old wooden chariot. His arrival fulfilled a local prophesy and he became king of the city, (which henceforth bore the name of Gordium), and ruler over all of Phrygia.

In gratitude to Zeus, Gordius dedicated the venerable relic of the chariot to the temple and then tied a huge, complex, multiple knot attaching the chariot's draw pole to its yoke. At some later point, a prophecy sprang up about this curious, elaborate knot: whoever could untie it would one day rule all of Asia.

Alexander the Great came to Gordium in the second year of his famous campaign against the Persian Empire. (This was three years after the oracle at Delphi had predicted that the new twenty-year-old king of Macedonia would be invincible in battle.) So far Alexander had lived up to this celebrated prediction but, at that moment, circumstances and events were combining to turn drastically against him.

The facts were that he was very close to running out of money to pay his troops, and a new, energetic commander-in-chief of the Persian forces in Asia Minor, a Greek mercenary named Memnon of Rhodes, was achieving victory after victory by fighting behind the Macedonian main forces. It appeared that, in a very short time, Alexander might well be overcome and, given that, perhaps it would be best if he turned around and went back to Greece. However, if he did so, wouldn't he prove that the Delphic oracle was wrong?

The huge skein of tangled tree-bark knot, standing as it did at a key-road junction, provides a superb metaphor for Alexander's own blocked state of mind at this critical juncture. Will he ignore the knot and its spectacular prophesy (that whoever unties it will win sovereignty over all of Asia), and return with his army to Greece? That would be the rational choice. Or will he face the challenge—a radical gesture many of us seem to shy away from—awaiting him with the knot?

As Alexander and his attendants make their way up to the acropolis, a large crowd of Macedonians and Phrygians follow, impelled by something more than mere curiosity. Surrounded by expectant onlookers, Alexander struggles energetically but helplessly with the labyrinthine tangle of rope. After a long while, the young king's usual self-assurance seems to weaken. At last he gives up. According to Alexander's historian Arrian, "He stood silent in thought for a while but he couldn't work out how to undo it."

Picture the shift: a king, a conqueror, full of the hero's impetuous *furie*, surrenders his conscious drive. He chooses to silence his critical voice, humble his ego, face the fear of not knowing. His greatness is in having the courage to admit the critical impasse: his conscious mind cannot solve this problem. Clearly, "something other" must happen.

Inhabiting Your Unease

Breathe out three times. Imagine yourself like Alexander, daring to inhabit your ambivalence, unrest, or emptiness, and to feel it. Breathe out once. Allow yourself to plunge below the surface problem into an open space. Describe the space and how you move in it. What is attracting you?

When the conscious mind acknowledges its failure and gives up trying to solve the problem, there is room for the emotions to be felt. This does not mean that the conscious mind goes to sleep. Instead it relinquishes center stage and steps aside to place itself in the observer's position.

It chooses to suspend its instinctive judgment, to quiet its natural drive for resolution. Think of this maneuver of the conscious mind as a ploy, a trick that the conscious mind plays on itself to get out of the way, exactly as in a tango *à deux* the man will turn away to leave room for his partner to shine.

Try it: you will see that ambivalence won't disturb you in quite the same way when you are no longer under pressure to perform. Just allow yourself whatever emotion you feel and acknowledge your experience, whether it means "I feel frustrated and humiliated" or "I love two women," or simply "I don't know." This allows you to sink into the body of the experience, the domain of the subconscious mind, where two seemingly opposite tendencies can co-exist. It is in this cauldron of paradox that "something other" can emerge.

MOVEMENTS OF THE SUBCONSCIOUS MIND

No longer constrained by the pedestrian means of travel, logic, and linearity, your mind is now free: it can leap, somersault, associate, invent, compose, or dissolve at will. The sibylline part of yourself, like a child released from school, explodes into movement. At first chaotic, this movement soon takes on a pattern, a direction: the child, having burst out of the building, pirouettes a few times, runs erratically in different directions, and is last seen skipping in and out between trees as he moves deeper into the forest.

What does the Alexandrian part of your mind do while this is happening? It watches with dawning amazement.

> *I have a feeling that my boat*
> *has struck, down there in the depths,*
> *against a great thing.*
> *And nothing Happens! Nothing . . . Silence . . . Waves . . .*
> *Nothing happens! Or has everything happened,*
> *and we are standing now, quietly, in the new life?*
> "OCEANS," JUAN RAMON JIMENEZ
> (TRANSLATION BY ROBERT BLY)

A new life appears, one fantastically different from the old, dull grind of rationality. The boat sits at the bottom of the ocean, oh, suspended grace! And the child? He is now deep in the forest and, stooping to smell a flower, he chats with a squirrel and basks in a patch of sunlight. Birds fly, trees swish in the wind, the child sings.

Curiously, being both minds at once, you are the conscious mind amazed as new pattern and directions emerge, *and* the subconscious mind at play, skipping in the woods! Observer and participant all in one—a paradox? Yes, but that is just what the field of experiencing is all about! Two aspects of ourselves can co-exist peacefully. Is that not worth facing your fears to explore?

THE NEW LIFE

Does this solve the problem? The poet says "everything has happened." But he is only a poet, notoriously unpractical, shall we believe him? Alexander must still unknot the Gordian knot. Let's listen to the end of the story.

Alexander stands silently confronting the knot in the temple plaza as murmurs and cries of encouragement come to him from the surrounding spectators. Of what happens next even (his historian) Arrian says: "I can speak with no confidence on this."

Maybe the poet knows more. If we allow ourselves the latitude to reconstruct what happened to Alexander, let us surmise that, in his mind, he plunges below the rational, to the "feeling" field. This he had done once before when, at the start of his flamboyant career, he went down into the darkness of the Pythia's cave at Delphi to encounter himself through her oracular saying.

In this inner sanctum Alexander is reminded, as the Pythia's voice once told him, that he is invincible. Here he is completely secure in his knowledge of what his life purpose is. This touches the one emotion that will surely motivate Alexander: his passionate ambition to fulfill his life's purpose. Instead of knowing rationally how to undo the knot, he "sees" *to what intent* he must apply himself. Beyond the cold fires of reasoning, the burning fire of ambition triggers the simple, clean way.

And while we do not know what vision/voice was vouchsafed to Alexander at this point, we *do* know that, raising his head, he suddenly shouts out, "What difference does it make *how* I loosen it?" draws his sword and, in one tremendous stroke, slashes through the Gordian knot. The tangle falls apart, laying wide open the road to Asia. None of his predecessors who had faced the challenge of the knot had thought of doing that. The subconscious is a revolutionary mind!

After cutting the Gordian knot, Alexander never looked back. Just weeks afterward, news came that his enemy Memnon had suddenly taken sick and died. Then, in November, the Macedonian army won a great battle against the Persian imperial army on the River Pinarus near the northeast corner of the Mediterranean coast. This victory opened the way for Alexander to remove the Persian navy from the war by occupying its ports. It also meant that, beginning with Egypt, he now had access to the great treasure troves of the East.

* * *

THE ENTWINING OF LOOKING AND DREAMING

What, you may well ask, is the difference between this oracular "Waking Dream" such as we have surmised Alexander spontaneously experienced, and the Guided Exercises which were your seventh task to practice? Remember how the Guided Exercises always start with a clearly circumscribed induction? Here we have the opposite: a mass of entanglements having no beginning or end, ambivalence that is caught in an either-or state, unease that has no name, emptiness, despair, or simply—what next?

In this case, the question is: what is the question? The Waking Dream is not the precise, directed tapping into the Source we learned to practice with the exercises, but an open-ended exploration of the imaginal field.

Yet how to explore this when our willful directives have been silenced? Here is a phenomenon worth contemplating: like our tango partners, our two minds cannot operate in isolation without creating the very knots we are speaking of. Each needs the other to reverse its respective, natural activity: the conscious mind must step back and watch, the subconscious must appear where it was hidden.

Let's call this a feedback loop: the "looking" of the conscious mind activates the "unfolding" of the subconscious. Without the eye of the conscious mind, the subconscious would not only remain hidden, but unmoving, entangled, knotted.

Yes, there is a subconscious Gordian knot that has so far remained hidden from our discourse. But here it is offered up for our contemplation and, as we "look," the imaginal field begins to move, unfold, take shape, like a flower opening its petals to the warmth of the sun. As discussed in chapter 1, it is this phenomenon that chaologists (those who study chaos and order) call "strange attractors."

That is exactly what we are out for: fully experiencing, as observing participants, the "order" emerging out of chaos. When we step aside we liberate a "chaotic" explosion of the subconscious while, *from* our looking, (like from a feedback loop), there comes a regulating movement. This is the "order" that "looking," (being always in search of a pattern), calls forth from the subconscious mind. Here is the new life that will effectively cut your Gordian knot.

PRACTICING WAKING DREAM

Are you feeling conflicted about something? Are you in difficulty? Are you unsure about what to do next? Are you simply curious as to who you are? Here is what you do.

Waking Dream

Breathe out three times. Imagine that you are standing in a meadow. Start by seeing and sensing everything that is in the meadow, the grass, flowers, insects, trees, other animals, people, habitations. Look up at the sky. What does it look like? Where is the sun in relation to you? What time of day is it? Sense everything as acutely as you can: the scent of the grass, the flowers, the touch of warmth from the sun, the breeze if there is any. Hear the insects, other animals, voices, wind. Even taste something if there is something you feel like tasting. The important thing is for you to be in your sensory body as much as possible. Breathe out once. Look around: What attracts you? Do you want to go there? Let yourself move as you wish. Your only role is to go along with what you sense and see yourself doing. Breathe out once. Follow the movement (remember you are both looking

and participating) wherever it leads. If it takes you up the hill, go there, if it takes you into a small hut, go for it. Remember, you are exploring. If you are frightened, the fear will make you back off, climb a tree, find reinforcements, or simply stop. But don't abandon the exploration, return to it until you can say, like the poet, "everything has happened" and "I am now standing quietly in the new life." You will know when that happens for you will feel satisfied, content, and ready to end this exercise. Breathe out once. Open your eyes and, remembering to ground yourself, sense the soles of your feet firmly on the ground, and your body in the chair.

What do you do with what just happened? Tell it to yourself out loud backwards. Then immediately write it down forward in your Waking Dream book. (This should be a separate book or folder that you have created specifically for this purpose.) Do not try to interpret what you have seen. Simply live with the images. They have a charge that, like the words of a sibyl's prophesy, have the power to motivate you. Be patient. You may not cut the Gordian knot as incisively as Alexander did. But then, you also may.

GORDIAN KNOTS OF
THE SUBCONSCIOUS

Shall we deny that Gordian knots of the subconscious exist as well? Those sudden unlooked-for eruptions of the subconscious mind, those unexpected shocking, jarring, or delightfully naughty associations: images of lopping off the feet of your boss, of hurling your kid into a pond, of tongue-to-tongue delight with your best friend's husband, of daggers in your heart—what are we to do with them? Or the repeated dream images that leave us with an unanswered, maybe troubling, question?

If left unattended and unexplored, these will soon become our hidden Gordian knots. We could call them repressed emotions, as the Freudians would, but I prefer to "see" them as flowers drooping for want of care. Soon we may have a desolate garden, a wasteland. How do we handle our unattended flowers? We take care of them by watering them with our "seeing": in other words, we look at them.

Addressing Your Unattended Dream Images

Breathe out three times. Return to your dream image (of night or day) and watch it. Allow it to move, unfold, take shape or change shape in any way it wishes. If it remains unmoving, address it verbally, touch it, or take something from it. (For instance, take the hat off its head, or touch it with your index finger.) Continue to watch until you sense completion. Do not worry about recognizing when it is complete, you will know it when it happens.

Thus we see there are two ways to initiate the Waking Dream: you either start with an open space or else with a current dream image that you want to explore. Either way, the motivation for exploration is an unease that exists that cannot be resolved by the conscious mind. Try to explore sparingly, but whenever you need to. You are learning, through practice, to dance the tango of the two minds. You may find it easier to practice all of this with a Waking Dream therapist, but if you remember always to play, and to keep the play open-ended, you can venture out alone. Enjoy your explorations: they are revealing you to yourself.

At this point in the game, it is clear you are committed to seeing the truth. The Waking Dream not only helps you in that elucidation but, much more than that, it allows you to see, revealed before your very eyes, the hidden treasures, richness, unending inventiveness, and abundance of your inner being. Just being showered with the contents of your inner cornucopia can effectively cut a Gordian knot, allowing you to go on to conquer your Asia then move on to bigger and better things.

* * *

Suddenly the dull world of your life has taken on marvelous hues, amazing shapes, unexpected twists—the garden is blooming! You have become an expert tango dancer. You are changing beyond recognition. Are you now willing, and strong enough, to look at the sad past, that still-untended garden? Think what may happen if you shower the past with your new richness. It, too, may become "something other" in the light of your attentive seeing. Are you ready to change the past? This will be your tenth task.

A QUICK REFERENCE GUIDE TO CHAPTER 9 EXERCISES

Inhabiting Your Unease (p. 138)

Breathe out three times. Dare to inhabit your ambivalence, unrest, or emptiness, and to feel it. Breathe out once. Allow yourself to plunge below the surface problem into an open space. Describe the space and how you move in it. What is attracting you?

Waking Dream: Exploring Your Subconscious Field (p. 142)

Breathe out three times. Imagine that you are standing in a meadow. See and sense everything that's in the meadow. Breathe out once. Look around. What attracts you? Follow the movement where it leads. Explore until you feel satisfied, content, and ready to end this exercise. Breathe out once. Open your eyes. Recount to yourself the Waking Dream backwards, with open eyes. Ground yourself by sensing that the soles of your feet are firmly on the ground, and your body rests firmly in its chair.

Addressing Your Unattended Dream Images (p. 144)

Breathe out three times. Return to a dream image (from the night or day) and watch it move and unfold to manifest new configurations until you sense completion. If the image doesn't move, address it verbally, touch it, or take something from it.

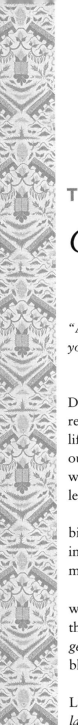

TEN

Changing the Past

"And you shall remember that you were a slave in Egypt and God took you out with a mighty hand and an outstretched arm."

DEUTERONOMY 5:15

Do you think we can remember our past? Look back. You probably remember the peaks and the valleys, the joys and the pains, of your past life in the same way that a gardener looking at his garden in bloom picks out the most magnificent blossoms and, to *his* eyes, the most disturbing weeds. He will, as he walks in his garden, also lay eyes on a particular leaf here, a petal there, or a vista that particularly pleases or strikes him.

So it is with memory. Memory is selective. It happily recognizes the big joys, stays amazed at a miraculous event, remembers some meaningless details, but if you examine it honestly you will find that your most frequent memories are memories of unhappiness.

Unfortunately, it is here that our memories most often get stuck. True, we can be stuck remembering a happiness we lost, but it is regret and loss that motivate us to spend time with the memory, not happiness. *Mostly we get stuck in the unhappiness.* As Tolstoy said, "All happy families resemble each other, each unhappy family is unhappy in its own way."

Happiness has no story. We prefer the drama, the tragedies, the pain. Like pigs to the trough, we are drawn by what the French call *le miel de la douleur* ("the honey of pain"). What attracts us so much to pain? Could it be that a current part of us is still stuck in the mud back there? We are not stuck in the past mud, for that doesn't exist anymore, but in the *image* of the past mud, with its self-perpetuating emotional charge. This current part of ourselves still hurts, and still cries out for help.

Time is cyclical, but for us it appears linear. We have a beginning and an end. We are doomed to die. Unfortunately, as we get older, it also feels for many of us as if there's a huge dump pile pushing at our backs, getting larger each moment. The future is frightening and the past is catching up with us, threatening to destroy us. Where do we go to hide? We cannot escape our future.

Can we escape our past?

* * *

EXPULSION FROM THE GARDEN OF EDEN

In the Bible the very first story about people (after they have been created) is a story of innocence lost. It is also the very first "story" in our personal pasts. Is it our destiny to follow in Adam and Eve's footsteps? Even in the Garden of Eden where abundance reigned, "Of every tree of the Garden, you may freely eat," one restriction existed: "But of the tree of the knowledge of good and bad, you must not eat thereof; for on the day you eat of it, you shall surely die" (Genesis 2:16–17).

Can you hear your mother saying, "You can do anything you want in my kitchen, just don't put your fingers near the fire!" Clearly, your mother made that rule out of love for you. So too did God make *His* rule out of love for mankind.

Here is Eve, a most perfect, harmonious, clear being; here are you, a fresh, innocent child. What happens? In Hebrew, the word for "snake" is *nachash,* which also means seducer, magician. What does the snake say to persuade Eve? "You will be like God, knowing good and bad" (Genesis 3:5) if you eat of the fruit.

Isn't that exactly what Eve wants to be, *like* God? When you were young, didn't you want to be just like your mother and, just like her, be able to put your hands near the fire? Emulation is a very persuasive and seductive argument when you are young and inexperienced. But, to keep you out of danger, obedience is required.

What happens next? You get burnt. You hurt. How can this happen to you and not to your mother? Innocence is injured. Suddenly you feel different, bad, exiled and, like Eve, expulsed from the garden of your oneness and separated from the one being you love and trust. *Separation is the first wound.*

Worse, you are confused. If something is *good* for Mother, why is it *bad* for you? You can't figure it out, good or bad, just as Eve couldn't when she ate of the fruit that held the confusing mixture of both good and bad. While you are ingesting the forbidden fruit, how are you going to be able to tell good and bad apart?

MIXING

Paradoxically, the consequence of separation is its opposite: mixing. Remember your busy dreams, filled with disquiet, restlessness, longing, but also with some good moments? They are busy because they are mixed. In them is some good and some bad. You can't quite tell the difference.

Go back to those painful events you remember: you love your father but, against his wishes, you borrow his camera (so you can do "just like him") and then you break it. You disobeyed him, things went terribly wrong, and he punished you. Result: you're filled with fear, ("I'm so sorry, I didn't mean it! Please, please!") but also you're feeling anxious about the consequences ("What will Father do to me?"). You love him and he punishes you.

How can he do this to you? Your innocence is deeply wounded. How are you going to sort out this inner turmoil? Your confusion could still be with you today. If it is, you are still living in a bad dream.

We now go to the second story of the Bible, where things get worse. Adam and Eve have been expelled from the Garden, and their sons, Cain and Abel, are making offerings to God. After they have made their offerings, it is clear that God prefers Abel to Cain.

Why is this so? Why does God prefer Abel to Cain? Everything seems very unfair to Cain: he has been punished with exile from the Garden for something his *parents* did, and this has made him justifiably angry. Being angry with God, Cain's offering to Him is made half-heartedly. God makes it clear that He is displeased with this half-hearted offering, and this doesn't sit well with Cain. "This annoyed Cain exceedingly" (Genesis 4:5).

Finding no resolution for his anger, Cain lets his frustration build. Finally he takes a stone, throws it at his brother, and kills him.

Now this is no longer a busy dream! Here is a nightmare! "You shall become a vagrant and a wanderer on earth" (Genesis 4:12). Like Cain, if something similar should happen to us, would we not be fearful for our safety, trying to hide, wandering aimlessly, knowing no tranquility? Are these not the emotions that are evoked by nightmares?

Later, Cain's descendant Lamech, mistaking the restless Cain for an animal, kills him. In his guilt, Lamech strikes his hands together and kills his own son. "Have I slain a man by my wound and a child by my bruise?" Lamech then laments (Genesis 4:23).

With these stories we can see how the original pain of separation (Eve's innocent disobedience) created *fear* and *anxiety* which led to Cain's *anger* and *frustration* (and murderous rage), which led to the further tragedy of Lamech (by accident and thus innocently) killing his own son (for which he was punished by his wives by their estrangement of him), causing *guilt* and *resentment*.

Imagine you are so angry with your father that you want to kill him. You make up all sorts of stories in your mind about how to do the deed. Then, if something bad happens to him, you feel terribly guilty. Guilt kills off your spontaneity, your "son." The flow of creativity stops and "your wives," i.e., your imagination, deny you their comfort. Resentment, like a blocked sewage, keeps gurgling up the same mess. Now, this is a recurring dream!

Fear and anxiety, anger and frustration, guilt and resentment; these are the dreadful mix-ups arising from the original wound of separation. They cause us to hide from the presence of the loved one ("and the man and his wife hid from HaShem, God, among the trees of the Garden" Genesis 3:8) to cover ourselves up—and soon we are hidden even from ourselves! We ignore our pain, creating elaborate complicated cover-up "stories" to mask it to ourselves and others. And our pain, thus deeply buried, is left to cause us unending misery.

SORTING OUT THE GOOD FROM THE BAD

Colette always forbade her students to use the word "confusion." Yet who can deny we were often confused, mixed-up, restless, unhappy, and stuck? That was why (at first) we went to her. Was her forbidding us to "be confused" yet another wounding of our innocence?

Clearly we live in a world where all things are separate and where, at the same time, "all things cleave to one another, the pure and the impure." Living in the world as we do, how are we to sort out the confusing mix of good and bad that the world, and our experience of it, contains? In other words, can we distinguish between what is *kosher* (fit for consumption) and what is *taref* (impure)?

By asking us to be specific and to describe exactly what was *in* the mix of our (confused) emotions, Colette was giving us a clue and a test. In the same way, Psyche was given a clue and a test by her mother-in-law Aphrodite when, as one of the tasks Psyche had to accomplish before she could return to her husband Eros, she was told to sort out all the grain Ceres kept to feed her innumerable pigeons.

 ### Sorting Out the Good Grain from the Bad

Breathe out three times. Imagine that you are faced with a huge pile of grain to sort out. Your job is to separate the good grain from the bad grain, creating two distinct piles. How do you go about accomplishing your task?

How successful were you? Psyche was helped by the fact that Eros wanted her back as badly as she wanted him, so he had instructed some nearby ants to take care of the impossible job of sorting for her. Ants are notoriously industrious, patient animals, who never stop working. As you may have guessed, this is work that is never quite done.

However evolved we are, however spiritual and elevated, still-alien emotions will insinuate themselves into all our relationships, trying to sabotage us. Should we therefore despair and give up the seemingly impossible task of trying to identify, in order to transform, our negative emotions? Or should we, like the disciplined, hard-working ant, persevere?

Think about what happens if you *don't* persevere. Your stored-up fears and angers become like the contents of a house that is never aired or cleaned, with things accumulating till they make it difficult, if not impossible, to live there. Unresolved emotions and thwarted desires crowd our minds, pushing against us, intruding on our present, muddying our vision of the future. Isn't it time we did something about them?

HOW EMOTIONS FROM THE PAST AFFECT US

Before we get to the actual work of sorting out the past and doing something to correct it, I want to examine some of the deceptively powerful forces we have to struggle with when we try to wrestle with a past that haunts us.

Let me tell you something about why there is so much resistance, both conscious or subconscious, to letting go of deeply buried pain. Suppose at an early age you were abandoned by an alcoholic father, then raised by an anxious and terrified mother who yelled at you all the time. Do you think you are going to grow up seeing the *goodness* in life?

No. Instead, your body will more likely be chronically contracted against abandonment, armored against anxiety. While this may accurately express your feelings towards the kind of world you experienced as a child, this instinctive raising of psychological armor never really protects you.

For one thing, it makes you more vulnerable to having your emotional "reaction buttons" pressed by people you meet who exhibit aggressiveness, or alcoholism, or instability, just like your parents did so long ago. *Your acute sensitivity to these people has its origins in your sense that they provide you with something you are used to, something you recognize.*

This pull of the familiar is so strong that it makes you forget, at first, that these are the same people who also bring you rejection and humiliation. "This time will be different," you tell yourself, but before you know it you are enthralled and captivated by the bad dream you have learnt too well how to live in.

This bad dream is hard to wake up from, for the past has taught you that this bad dream is the only "reality" there is. Because of the law of "strange attractors" (see chapter 1) you have seen your bad dream replay itself over and over: you are abandoned by every man/woman you enter into a close relationship with.

There will be times when this unrewarding pattern makes you so uncomfortable that you decide to do something about it. If you take steps that actually lead to some change, however, you will make an unpleasant discovery that will very likely bring your new life to a screeching halt.

I'm talking about the great, often unacknowledged fear that we all have of the unknown. The threat of this fear, combined with the gravity-like tug of our formative years, makes it extremely difficult to break the pattern of our bad-dream rut. How can you possibly open up to something new, to something other than what you have always believed is a fact: life is difficult, poverty a given, loneliness your lot. Life has proven this to you again and again.

If I were to tell you it can be otherwise, you wouldn't believe me. You might even feel insulted, thinking I was ignoring or denigrating the injury you feel was done to your innocence. Yet I am going to tell you *just* that: you *can* change these patterns in your life.

You have come this far. You know you are not powerless. You know you are the co-creator of your life. Use this knowledge now to see that when you allow yourself to be enthralled by a dream of abandonment, you inevitably call for its complement: the person who will abandon you.

We all do this. We force our dream "stories" onto the world where they act like hungry mouths waiting to be filled. If I am a glove, a hand will reach in and fill me. If I am a dark cave, a beast will come and crouch in me. Only by stretching out of my cave-like posture can my "story" change.

If I *do* stretch out, suddenly the cave is gone and the beast has nowhere to crawl to. He will either change his "story" to fit my new configuration, transforming out of his beast-like stance in the process, or he will go and find another cave.

Can you risk changing your "story"? Give up being abandoned? Dare to face the unknown in order to let your new configuration emerge? You have done it with night dreams. Why not try it with the past?

THE FIRST STEP: ACKNOWLEDGING YOUR PAIN

The first wound was separation: another word for it is "stopping." You were stopped, denied fulfillment of your longing to be One with your mother, with God. Return to the diagrams I drew for you in chapter 2. When your instincts are stopped, when you are separated from the accomplishment of your deepest desire, your unused energy (intended to *fulfill* your desire) gets shunted, igniting instead your reactions (the emotions of fear and anger, figure 3). When fear and anger in *their* turn have no place to go, they stagnate in a pool of muddied waters. Within those confines they grow restless, agitate, turn into anxiety, frustration, guilt, resentment (figure 4).

Soon more *fleurs du mal*—disappointment, depression, hopelessness, despair, cowardice, laziness, stupidity, ignorance—make their appearance. How can you, at this point, acknowledge your pains, since their colors have bled into one huge mass of muddied waters? How can you sort them out? We have already introduced the Jewish concept of Tshuva, or return, in chapter 5.

Your goal is to return to the place of harmony where energies flow easily and fluidly, but before you can do that, you must first return to the *source* of your pain. This is how you do it.

Reversing on Fear and Anxiety

Breathe out three times. Return back to the first time you felt fear and anxiety. How old are you? What is the event? Where is it located? Who are the people involved? Allow yourself to feel the pain as you felt it then. Do not shy away from it. Acknowledge your pain. You don't want to do it the injury of separating from it again. Feel it completely. Breathe out once. Move forward to the next event you can remember where you felt fear and anxiety. Do so for as many events as you can remember, at this time, where you felt fear and anxiety. Thus move forward in time till you reach the present moment.

Feel your pain! You can't help a suffering child by *telling* him to stop crying! First you must comfort him. If you don't comfort him, he may stop crying to make you happy, but he won't be *at one* with you. The separation will still be very much there.

Eventually you think the crisis is over, since his tears have stopped flowing. However, his tears have stopped flowing because they have *crystallized*. Soon he's living in a "room of tears." Your task is to find *your* crystallized tears and allow them to flow. Your "seeing" is the comforting parent of your tears. When your tears flow, the river can return to the ocean. Tshuva has begun.

TIKKUN AND PURIFICATION

Where is the first ocean? In your mother's womb where you started, in God's clear waters where the Garden rested. "A river issues forth from Eden to water the Garden" (Genesis 2:10). To return to this perfect place, allow your pain to be swept away, in the flow of your tears, in joyful anticipation of Tshuva. The resonance of pain, the "story," is what you must sweep away.

The Jews have another concept called *Tikkun*. Tikkun means "correction." You can now begin to apply correction to the past.

Tikkun Exercise

Breathe out three times. Imagine that you have a strong garden broom, the old kind made of branches. You also have a powerful garden hose and a knife, in case you need them. Return back through all the places you just visited in your last exercise. Sweep each place clear of the resonance of fear and anxiety, sweep it out to the left. If this doesn't work, (if you still feel enthralled), use your hose. If necessary, cut the resonance out with your knife. If there are people involved you don't want in your life anymore, sweep them out too. Remember it all goes to the left. Do that till you reach the first memory of pain. Then, having swept its resonance out, return to be in your mother's womb. If that is not comfortable, see yourself bathing in God's clear waters on this Earth. You are His perfect child again. You can now be born again, corrected, renewed, perfected.

You have purified yourself as much as you can today. Tomorrow you will do this again, and again the next day. More events, more details, will surface out of the muddy waters to be cleared out. You are sorting out the good from the bad.

GROUNDING YOURSELF IN
THE NEW PAST

Return is not complete until you bring your new self back into the world, into the present moment. Although we always inhabit the present moment, we are not often present to it. How could we be truly present when a pool of fear and anxiety was pressing on us, claiming our attention? Now you can enter and journey forth from the Garden of Eden—as did Rabbi Akiba—to the present moment where you can live as fully as your new freedom allows.

A New Past, New Present

Breathe out once. Imagine being born again perfectly. See yourself journeying through all the places where the difficult events of your life, as you have identified them above, took place. But now they are free of the old resonance. The facts may be the same, but you are not ensnared by them anymore. You pass unfettered, free, thus creating a new past. Pass through each place till you come to the new present. Live it fully.

THE NEW FUTURE

Now your past and your present are new. What about the future? The old "story" is gone. True, the facts remain, but you see them differently, you feel them differently. You are no longer a victim, an innocent oppressed. Cleared of its emotional entanglements, your "story" can relax and sink to a hitherto-unknown depth of feeling.

While you may lose some of the driven linearity of your story, you will probably experience a new luminosity, a sense of timelessness that we tend to associate with happy moments. Suddenly your vision of the future is given wings! You can leap to a revolutionary new view of what it will be. But remember: do not force anything. This is not a *willful* process. Allow your dreaming once again to show you the way.

A New Future

Breathe out once. See yourself in your new future. See yourself in a month's time. What do you look like? Where are you? Are you alone or with others? What are you doing? What is the feeling? Breathe out once. See yourself in three months' time. What do you look like now? Breathe out once. In a year's time; breathe out once. In five years' time. Breathe out once. Return to your new present, feel yourself in your new life, with your new past and your new future anchoring you firmly in the new present.

Give yourself time to do these exercises. They are called "Reversing the Past." Do them every day for three weeks, then stop for a week. If you still feel you haven't exhausted all of your memories of *fear* and *anxiety*, start another set (for three weeks, then stop a week), or move on (you can always return to *fear* and *anxiety* at a later time) to *anger* and *frustration.*

Don't give up till you have exhausted every possible memory of *anger* and *frustration.* It may take months, even years. And why not? They took years to build. Then move on to *guilt* and *resentment.*

You may find you resonate more to *guilt* and *resentment* than to *fear* and *anxiety.* You are free to change the order, only don't stop doing them until all of your past pain is exhausted.

HOW TO DEAL WITH THE IMMEDIATE PAST

Having cleared out the old past, are you going to allow new pains to accumulate? You have been sorting out the good from the bad. Now you must learn to do it in the moment. There are two simple exercises you can do in the moment. Try this one first because, once you have learned to do it with closed eyes, you can do it with open eyes and no one will notice what you are doing.

The Black Triangle

Breathe out, seeing your exhalation as a dark smoke that gathers in front of you in the shape of a triangle of black smoke. Continue to breathe out the black smoke till your breath becomes clearer, than transparent. Now breathe strongly onto the triangle, breaking it into thousands of pieces. Breathe out a second time, seeing the pieces dissolving. Breathe out a third time, seeing that the atmosphere in front of you is totally cleared up. Breathe out and open your eyes.

If you need an even quicker clearing, then see yourself breathing out three times, exhaling the smoke and, with it, all that disturbs you.

Here is another fast way of dealing with the immediate past.

Sweeping the Dead Leaves

Breathe out three times. You are standing on the porch of an old country cottage. The floor is covered with dead leaves. Using a sturdy garden broom sweep them into a heap then, breathing out once, sweep the heap off the porch to the left. Breathe out and open your eyes.

In order that my students will remember to practice this exercise, I give them a miniature broom, a reminder that they can keep in view on their office desk or at home. It is so easy to forget and to let our "story" creep up on us again. The catastrophic voice, the anxious image, the guilty posture, all must be "seen" and acknowledged, and the resonance swept off to the left.

If you do this consistently your old resonances will fade. If you forget, you will revert back to your old ways because nothing stays static in the dream world, just as gravity will pull us down if we do not practice standing up straight. You will either choose the good, or collapse back into the confusion. If you choose the good, a new life can dawn for you. Will you choose it?

* * *

Clearing out the past was an arduous task. Be sure you have thoroughly examined every last memory you can dredge up, for your next task will be the most difficult: anchoring yourself in the new life you have chosen. Are you ready to become a *baal tshuva*, a "Master of return or response"? Are you ready to perfect your Life Plan? This will be your eleventh task.

A QUICK REFERENCE GUIDE TO CHAPTER 10 EXERCISES

Sorting Out the Good Grain from the Bad: To Clear Confusion (p. 150)

Breathe out three times. Imagine that you are faced with a huge pile of grain to sort out. Your job is to separate the good grain from the bad grain and place them in two separate piles. How do you go about accomplishing your task?

Reversing on Fear and Anxiety (or Anger and Frustration, or Guilt and Resentment) (p. 153)

To clear and change the past, reverse on either of the three following pairs of emotions, in whichever order you want: a) fear and anxiety, b) anger and frustration, c) guilt and resentment. Breathe out three times. Return to the first time you felt fear and anxiety. What was the event? Where in your body is it located? Who were the people involved? Feel the emotional pain. Breathe out once. Move forward to the next event you can remember where you felt fear and anxiety (or anger and frustration or guilt and resentment). Do so for as many events as you can remember where you felt fear and anxiety, etc. Then move forward in time until you reach the present moment.

Tikkun Exercise (p. 154)

Breathe out three times. Imagine that you have a strong garden broom. Return back through all the emotional places you have just visited, sweeping from those places out to the left all the resonances of fear and anxiety. If there are people involved you don't want in your life anymore, sweep them out to the left also. If the sweeping doesn't do it, use a powerful garden hose or a knife.

Continue back through all the places where you have identified fear and anxiety, until you reach the first memory. Having cleared that, return into your mother's womb, or see yourself bathing in God's clear waters on this Earth.

A New Past, New Present (p. 155)

Breathe out once. Imagine being born perfectly and journeying through all those places that have been swept clear of the old resonances. Pass, unfettered and free, creating your new past, until you come to your new present.

A New Future (p. 156)

Breathe out once. See yourself in your new future. See yourself in a month's time. What do you look like? Where are you? Are you alone or with others? What are you doing? What are you feeling? Breathe out once. See yourself in three months' time. What do you look like? Where are you? Breathe out once. See yourself in one year's time. What do you look like? Where are you? Breather out once. See yourself in five years' time. What do you look like? Where are you? Breathe out once. Return to your new present, feel yourself in your new life, with your new past and your new future anchoring you firmly in the new present.

The Black Triangle: So as not to accumulate negative residue, learn to clear pains as they appear in the moment (p. 157)

Breathe out, seeing your exhalation as a dark smoke that gathers in front of you in the shape of a triangle of black smoke. Continue to breathe out the black smoke until your breath becomes clearer, then transparent. Now breathe strongly onto the triangle, breaking it into thousands of pieces. Breathe out a second time, seeing the pieces dissolving. Breathe out a third time, seeing that the atmosphere in front of you is totally cleared up. Breathe out and open your eyes.

Sweeping the Dead Leaves (p. 157)

Breathe out three times. You are standing on the porch of an old country cottage. The floor is covered with dead leaves. Using a sturdy garden broom, sweep them into a heap then, breathing out once, sweep the heap off the porch to the left. Breathe out and open your eyes.

ELEVEN

The Master Game:
Perfecting the Life Plan

"Who is a hero? He who subdues his inclination."

AROT 4:1

"In returning and in rest you shall be saved; in quietness and in trust shall be your strength."

ISAIAH 30:15

There is an old kabbalistic belief that if just one Sabbath (day of rest) were observed by all the Jews in the world, the Messiah would come, bringing peace and harmony to our distraught and pain-filled lives. Short of having all the Jews perform together, can we bring into this world our "Inner Messiah?" *Can we give rise to love and goodness in place of reactivity and thwarted desires?*

You have learned to identify your claims, expectations, needs, and desires; to recognize your reactions. Are you going to allow yourself to be mastered by them? Or, learning from the great STOP! game of the Jews, (the Sabbath), will you perfect your dream work by catching your emotions as they arise in order to switch their energy in a "better" direction? Can you imagine converting emotions to feeling—anger to love, fear to courage, guilt to freedom?

The culmination of your life's work as a dreamer is visualizing and bringing heaven onto earth. When the goodness, love, and harmony of

161

heaven shine out from your heart into the world, they touch and trans-figure—not only your own life—but the lives of all those you encounter. As a true dreamer, one who has given direction to your dreaming energy, you can be one of the many beacons of light that help transform the world into a better place.

* * *

TRANSMUTING FEAR INTO VICTORY

Goliath was an impressive and seasoned warrior. He had been a "war-rior from his youth" (I Samuel 17:33). He stood "six cubits and a span," and was a huge man wearing a coat of mail and bronze greaves. His spear's head alone weighed six hundred shekels of iron. When the men of Israel saw this champion of the Philistines, "they fled from him and were sore afraid" (I Samuel 17:24). Just so does your fear appear in your dream images when you see it revealed for the first time—a giant of an ogre ready to belittle, diminish, and crush you.

Each of your emotions comes clothed in the nightmarish garb of its specific quality: a spitting dragon, an old hag, a greenish blob may be your anger, your spitefulness, your indolence. What you don't always remember is that emotions are only energy (see chapter 2) masquerad-ing under one guise or another. It is up to you to use your dreamer's magic wand to transmute these fearful images.

You have learned to re-enter your dreams in daytime conscious-ness, to face the fearful images that were revealed to you during your night dreaming. For the time being, however, you still haven't per-fected how to catch and transmute your emotions as they occur in the *daytime.* Your emotions still appear dangerous, repulsive, dismaying, even to you who live with them. Will you be like the men of Israel, "sore afraid," unwilling and unable to challenge your own monster emotions?

Goliath bleakly spells out the conditions for the Israelite warrior who chooses to fight with him: "If he be able to fight with me, and to kill me, then will we be your servants; but if I prevail against him, and kill him, then shall you be our servants and serve us" (I Samuel 17:9).

Only David, the smallest, the humblest, the youngest of the hosts of Israel, was willing to answer Goliath's challenge. Saul, seeing how puny

David was, dressed him in his own armor, but David wanted nothing to do with what was untried for him, and he took off the armor the king had given him. He was not pitting his strength against the giant's strength, for in that battle he would surely lose. David was going to *outsmart* Goliath.

David said to Goliath on the battlefield: "Thou comest to me with a sword, and with a spear, and with a shield: but I come to thee in the name of the Lord of hosts, the God of the armies of Israel, . . . that all the earth may know there is a God in Israel" (I Samuel 17:45–46).

A sling of the type shepherds use to herd the flock and protect it was David's simple weapon. One stone, landing between Goliath's eyes, felled the giant and in a single instant fear was transformed into victory. The men of Israel, so frightened a moment before, rose as one man to charge and overwhelm the Philistines.

It takes only an instant, a shift of seeing, for fear—the ogre—to become the servant to our kavanah. For as David said, "Is there not a cause" (I Samuel 17:29) to defend? The greatness of the living God of Israel was David's cause. Turning his eyes to his God's greatness, as all great dreamers do, David was able to *transmute* his energy. Suddenly there was a conduit, a pipeline, to conduct the energy sparked by fear to where it would most benefit: defending his God.

Imagine the firing of David's emotions as a discharge of electricity: just as electricity can be a dangerous commodity in and of itself, when it is properly channeled it will illuminate a city. This channeling of energy was David's kavanah. The city that is lit by it we'll call "feeling."

Why feeling? *What is the difference between emotion and feeling?* We have talked about this before, but let's explore the question further here. Generally there is little distinction made between emotion and feeling, but if you pay close attention you'll discern a radical difference. Close your eyes and take a look:

Distinguishing between Emotions and Feelings

Breathe out three times. Experience, sense, and then describe to yourself the movement of anger. Breathe out once. Sense how anger wants to project outward in a single concentrated thrust or direction. With your hand, sweep the anger out of your body to the left.

 *Breathe out once again. Now experience, sense, and then describe to yourself the movement of love. Breathe out once. Sense how love suffuses and envelopes your whole being before emanating from you in all directions. Stay with the feeling of love, see yourself as a star radiating the light of love in all directions.*

Emotion, as was described in chapter 2, is a *movement out*, a spark of electricity in reaction to an outer trigger, while feeling is a *state of being*. Just as electricity, having found its container—a light bulb for instance—fills and irradiates the light bulb, so does feeling glow and shine forth from us in all directions. That is why people who are in love look so radiant.

Having come to understand this distinction between feeling and emotion, can you now see that emotion is not a bad thing, certainly not something to suppress or feel guilty about? Rather, it is something for us to use, it is our trigger, it is essential. *We need the flame of emotion to light the fire of feeling.*

But remember, if we are not immediately attentive to the flame (of our emotion), and aware of what we want to use it for (lighting a fire), it could spark a conflagration. Unchecked emotion sparked panic in the hosts of Israel. In their fear, all they could envision was running away, causing a rout.

But David, the child, the dreamer, the lover, used the emotion of fear to propel himself toward greater things. As we, too, learn to change old tyrants into willing servants, as we transform and transmute our emotions into feeling, like David we will be crowned king of our emotions. *How, while distancing ourselves from our dreams of fear—the nightmares, the busy and recurring dreams that delude us into becoming the servants of our lesser being—do we anchor our souls in this great dream of kingship?*

IDENTIFYING YOUR MOST FREQUENTLY EXPERIENCED EMOTION

A friend once said to me: "Men and women are animals so long as they react. They only become human beings when they learn to respond."

Responding means transmuting emotions into feeling. How do we learn to *respond*?

Identifying Your Most Frequently Experienced Emotion

The first step is to become aware of your reactions. Remember that with your reaction to an outside stimulus, an emotion is sparked. If you have done your work, (in chapter 2) you have a little notebook in which you have, during one week, recorded all of your emotions. Go over your list. You will soon identify the emotion that comes back most frequently.

Suppose it is anger. Anger will be the emotion you focus on this month. Don't try to work with more than one emotion at a time as you will have your work cut out for you with one. You will see that as soon as you start focusing on a specific emotion, it acts like an animal cornered, endangered, stirred up. The next thing you know, it is acting out, just like Goliath who, emerging from behind the Philistines' ranks where he was hiding, goaded and screamed at the men of Israel.

When you start working with your anger, it will become more violent, unpredictable, and volatile. I tell you this not to frighten you but to let you know what might be coming. Being forewarned, you will not be upset or caught off-guard. When anger erupts, you will say: "Not to worry! That was to be expected!"

To keep the work effective, the length of time you work on an emotion is limited. This allows for greater focus and the gathering in of your energies to meet your goal. Once you have chosen the emotion you want to work with, how do you go about becoming like King David?

CATCH THE EMOTION WHEN IT OCCURS

Emotions are not thoughts. They are experiences. When you feel anger, your whole body is involved. Your heart beats faster, color rushes to your face or out of it. Your legs tremble. For each of us anger manifests in a slightly different way.

Do you know how anger manifests in your body? If you haven't identified its physical signs beforehand you may not be able to catch your anger when it first occurs. Isn't that strange? Anger is such a firecracker emotion one would think we'd be able to identify it immediately. And yet that is not always the case.

For instance, you are enjoying yourself at a dinner party, but as you leave you sense a surge of anger. You recognize that your anger has been simmering all through the diner party but you paid no attention to it. Also, you have no idea *why* you are angry.

Reversing to pinpoint the exact cause of your discomfort, you remember the nasty remark your friend made. Meanwhile, because you didn't identify your anger when it first happened, like a wave it has now washed over you and flooded you. At this point you have no choice but to wait patiently for it to recede. Hopefully the wave is small and you will not drown in it, latch onto it, or lose too much time processing it out of your system.

Wouldn't it have been better if you had caught your anger when it first reared its "ugly" head? You might have been able to do something about it then. We all seem to have a knack for living *à retardement*, as the French say, "in delayed time," instead of just simply living in the moment.

Becoming conscious of the exact unfolding of an emotion in your body will help you to recognize it the instant it appears. Here's how you do it:

Recognizing an Emotion in the Moment

Breathe out once. Imagine that you are experiencing intense anger. If you need to return to a moment of your past when you experienced anger, do so. Describe to yourself all the physical manifestations of your anger. Where do you feel it in your body? What color is it? What does it feel like—is it a pressure, contraction, dissolution, weakening, knotting? Find the right words to describe your sensations. When you can accurately describe them, sweep your sensations out of your body to the left. Breathe out and open your eyes.

SHIFT HAPPENS

What purpose is served in being acutely aware of what is happening to you *when* it is happening? Imagine that instead of being a passenger in the speeding train of your life, you are the switchman at the central switchboard. This, if you recall, is a dreaming maneuver. While you speed along in your train, you are also "considering," from the switchman's position, the train's direction.

Like the switchman, you are master of the switch board. If you look carefully you will see that your train is traveling on the track labeled "Anger." Because your train habitually journeys on that track, you haven't realized that you can *change* tracks; you can send your train speeding in another direction. All it takes is a flipping of the switch.

And yet, there is but one point in time when you can flip that switch: as the train comes into view just before it reaches the shunt. But how are you going to make that decision on the spur of the moment if you have no idea *where* you want to redirect your train? *In other words, you must come prepared, like the switchman, with new destination choices.*

Imagine sending your train to the destination known as "Love." Only with strong kavanah, your dreaming capacity to "see" something other than what it is used to, will you be able to make the switch on time. And remember, if you don't, the train will simply continue on its habitual track and you'll have to wait for another train to come along.

As in any functioning switchboard, the switch, (the "new destination" for your emotion), needs to be labeled. I labeled it "Love" to give you an example. But this shouldn't be randomly decided. It is best to choose a destination to suit your individual need. To label your new destination you must ask your dream body to help you.

Labeling the Switch

Breathe out three times. Imagine the completely opposite sensation from the sensation of anger you just experienced. Where is it in your body? What color is it? What does it feel like? Expansion, dilation, tingling, lightness, etc. . . . Give it a name, whatever is right for you, for instance: love, peace, harmony, balance, quiet. Your dreaming will tell you. Breathe out and open your eyes.

Remember, we cannot dispense with an emotion without replacing it with something better, in the same way that we cannot dispense with a bad habit without replacing it with another, better one. This is why so many people fail miserably in their efforts to stop smoking, overeating, getting chronically angry, or any number of other bad habits.

Where there is an empty space you must dream up something better or the empty space will fill up with the old dream again, and you, sadly, will be back where you started. There is no way to remain neutral in this process. As Goliath's statement made clear, it is a case of "fight like a warrior" to master your emotions, or let yourself be defeated by them and become their slave.

Only when you have identified and labeled the feeling which will subsume anger can you begin laying down the tracks that will conduct your energy to its new destination.

* * *

THE NEW DESTINATION

Soon after Potiphar, the Egyptian captain of the guard, bought Joseph, he was forced to recognize what a remarkable person his new slave was. Unfortunately, Potiphar's wife, a seductive, determined, and relentless woman, responded in her own way to Joseph's fine qualities. Like a bad habit, she would appear day after day and beg her husband's chief overseer to: "Lie with me!" (Genesis 39:12).

Can you imagine how Joseph must have felt? He must have been filled with conflicting emotions: fear, anger, resentment, and, if we are to believe the Talmudic sages, desire. As if to provoke fate, or so it would seem, he entered Potiphar's house one day when no man of the household was there.

Sure enough, "She caught hold of his garment saying, 'Lie with me!'" But, as the Talmudic sages tell us, at the moment when Joseph's closeness to Potiphar's wife was most overpowering, he "saw" his father's face at the window! (Sotah, 36b). That was enough to *flip*

Joseph's switch. "He left his garment in her hand, and he fled outside" (Genesis 39:12).

We know of the deep bond between Joseph and his father Jacob. In Joseph's moment of great temptation, when it seemed that desire would preempt his better self, Jacob, his heartland, his higher dream, the destination toward which he had been drawn all his childhood, asserted its claim. The energy of Joseph's desire "moved" away from Potiphar's wife to that "better" self which the vision of his father's face had re-ignited within him.

But that was *Joseph*! What if *you* don't have the gravitational pull of a Jacob in your life? *Where, in your moment of necessity, will you find the strength to flip the switch?*

SURNATURE

To think that we can invent a new destination on the spur of the moment is to be overly sanguine, although I'm not saying it can't happen. In moments of great adversity, people have re-invented themselves. These sudden and groundbreaking shifts, however, take a great toll on our psyche, and we can't count on them. Thus it is best to prepare the ground beforehand. This is what a good education does for us.

Just as our bodies are subject to the natural pull of gravity, our psyches are attracted to our more natural urges (desires and reactions). Yet even as we are giving in to our slumped bodies and our easily assuaged desires, all of us have an inner voice urging us to take another, better way.

As Goliath pointed out in the field at Ephesdammim, there is no neutral position; we are always being pulled in opposite directions. We have been given free will, the ability to choose whether to give in to the pull of Nature or rise above it to what the French call *Surnature*, i.e., "above Nature."

Let's say we've decided not to slump anymore but to hold our spine erect. This is all very well for us to decide, but Nature has other plans and we must *work* to make Surnature happen. Day after day we must train our bodies to counteract gravity: to push our feet and shoulders down, to strengthen our inner thigh muscles to elongate our spine. The next time we get pushed around in a crowd, the habit of elongation will serve us in good stead. Surnature has taken hold and we easily regain our balance.

Take Joseph again. After being exiled and sold into slavery, an acute sense of loss, grafted onto the already existing weight of his affection, duty, and habit as regards his father, would have etched Jacob's face more deeply into Joseph's heart and mind. When he was sorely tempted to give in to desire, the habit of returning to the "good" destination worked in his favor. That was Joseph's good fortune. But how, if *we* haven't had such education and experience, can we etch *our* new destination into our hearts and minds?

BUILDING KAVANAH

The realm of feeling has a broad range of points of application. *Since feeling is triggered by a response, it always comes from the heart realm.* Love, harmony, peace, quietude, openness, compassion, joy, mercy, kindness, goodness, grace, hope, happiness, courage, fortitude, perseverance, patience, and understanding are clearly of the heart. Clarity, precision, judgment, justified anger, justice, detachment, freedom are also of the heart, but they are combined with severity. (For instance, many people today appear to feel that it is *heartless* to discipline their child while, in the long run, of course it is a necessary part of loving care for a child.)

And what of David's allegiance to his God's greatness? Yes, that too is a heart response—just as your dream to excel in your studies, win the tennis championship, paint a masterpiece, or succeed in your business can be a heart response. Switching to a creative destination lifts you above the everyday humdrum of instinctual behavior and reactivity to a state of beingness.

In kabbalistic lore the destination is called simply "the Place" (*ha-Makom*).

> But if your heart runs, return to the place (ha-Makom), for
> that is the reason it is said, "And the angels run and return,"
> (Ezekiel 1:14) and on this matter a covenant was cut.
>
> SEFER YETZIRA 1:8

The secret hidden behind these words of the Sefer Yetzira, or Book of Creation, one of the most ancient and difficult of kabbalistic texts, is that the place to return to is ultimately God. We know this because one of the names of God is ha-Makom. Isaac the Blind gave form to this supreme intent which kabbalists call *devekut*, a word that translates as "cleaving" to, or communing with, God.

To cleave to God, if that is your wish, you must start with simple things. You have learned to ask your dream body what "better" destination to choose. But it is your physical body you must use to etch out the new destination. With its rhythms and habits, the physical body is easy to program. Instead of tricking ourselves beyond our instincts and

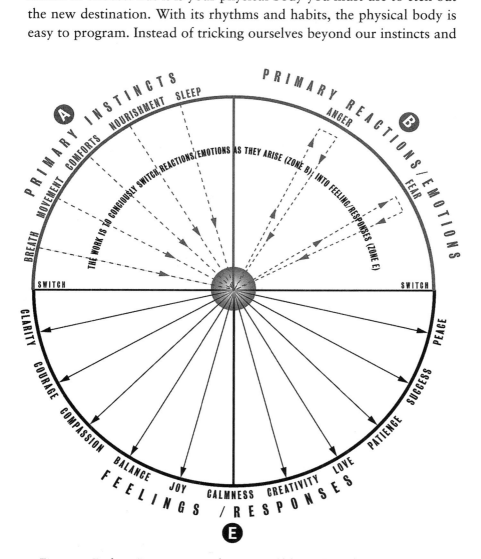

Figure 6. Feelings/Response. To free yourself from the habitual see-saw of movement between instincts and reactions, learn to switch to feelings/response by visualizing your feeling destination at the very moment that you are observing the beginning signs in yourself of a reaction/emotion.

habits, as we learned to do in chapter 6, here we are going to make use of the body's habit-forming nature to build Surnature.

For women this is easy; a woman's menstrual cycle is a natural and obvious timekeeper. We use the time in between menstruation (generally twenty-one days) for programming, the time the menstrual flow occurs (generally seven days) for the pause. But why a pause?

Imagine music without pauses. It would be a cacophony of noise. It's the same with the body: if you ate all the time your body wouldn't be able to tell when you were really hungry. The body only understands regularity if it is defined by pauses. To teach the body a new habit, to etch in its memory a "higher instinct," we need to conform to that simple physical law. You can teach anything to the body so long as you teach it in the regular intervals of natural rhythms (seven and multiples of seven are natural rhythms) of beats and pauses.

What about the men? What clock do they use? Since they don't have an obvious internal rhythm like women do, they must make do with external rhythms. Jewish men are taught to follow the rhythms of the moon. Each month at *Rosh Hodesh* they step outside to greet the new moon with songs and prayers. If you are a man, following the rhythms of the moon is easy and may work for you.

Get a calendar that includes the moon's phases, or watch the night sky. But if that seems too complicated, twenty-one days' programming, starting at *any* time of the month, will work also. Thus men's bodies become like women's in this regard: rhymed and easily trainable.

USING SOUNDS TO BUILD NEW DESTINATIONS

There are many ways to program yourself to build new destinations for your energy. Sound is one of the more powerful ways, mainly because there is a greater concentration of muscles around the throat area than anywhere else in the body. By making sounds we activate all those muscles. The sounds themselves vibrate within us, creating kinesthetic effects that vary depending on the nature of the sounds.

When the physical body is thus strongly activated, a synergy of sensations occurs that imprints the imaginal field with its particular pattern. You will find that the type of chanting I'm about to describe awakens all your senses—the auditory, the tactile-kinesthetic, the visual, the olfactory, the taste buds—in that declining order of intensity.

If you activate the physical body in a precise way at regular intervals, you will soon find out that the body gets hungry for the type of stimulation you have accustomed it to, at exactly those precise time intervals. The body, having become habituated to a particular pattern, can no longer do without it.

The great religions understood this perfectly when they instituted formal prayer three times a day, or five times a day for Muslims who add both chanting and the powerful effects of physical prostrations to their prayer. Religious rituals accomplish a function similar to ours, that of returning to a destination—in their case God—three or five times a day.

Food is another good example. You eat three times a day or five and, because you eat this frequently, think how often during the day food comes into your thoughts. If you have been habituated to pray to God three or five times a day, God will come into your thoughts more often than into those of someone who is not practicing daily prayer. Kabbalists call this process *devehkut*, or "cleaving." By its practice, kabbalists learn to cleave to God.

Our work, which I call the "Master Game," is to cleave to the imaginal field called "feeling," the realm of the heart response. As we develop the heart response we will naturally be brought to contemplate higher realms (Surnature), or God if that is our inclination.

CHANTING

When chanting, it is best to use a sacred language. Sacred languages are more closely related to the body experience that we want to convey than modern languages are. For instance, try chanting the sound "Aaa."

Chanting to Anchor Your "Feeling Destination"

Close your eyes. Chant the sound "Aaa." Take your time. Sense how the sound activates your body and describe to yourself all its physical effects. Then stop and watch. What name do you give to what you feel?

Did you feel how the sound "Aaa" expanded your chest area and opened up the heart center? The Hebrews knew this, that is why their word for love is "AHAVA." Note how there are three "A" sounds in AHAVA. Now close your eyes and try chanting the word "love." What happens in your chest area?

If you have observed, as I'm sure you have, that the chest area contracts when chanting the word "love" (instead of expanding), you will understand why it is wiser to use a sacred language such as Hebrew or Sanskrit for your chanting. I will provide a list of Hebrew words for you in appendix 2.

If this doesn't sit well with you, just use English words, for ultimately the most important thing is that you feel comfortable in the process. You will not have the *sounds* working for you but you will have the *intent*.

In our tradition, we chant words on three notes: "MiDoRe." The three-pronged tempo is very important, for three is an easily recognizable inner pattern. For instance, we remember three-step dances easily, and we tend to think in three movements: thesis, antithesis, synthesis.

Try playing "MiDoRe" on your piano keyboard, if you have one. If you aren't a musician, just sing the "Do Re Mi Fa So La Si Do" sequence to find and isolate the sound of "MiDoRe." What is important about this sound is that it does not simply go up or down, it moves from up to down to lesser up, a pattern that will activate your body because it is irregular. Again we remain within the parameters defined earlier in our search for new destinations: rhythm and activation.

Chanting on "MiDoRe"

Breathe out once. Chant the word "AHAVA" on the notes Mi (A), Do (HA), Re (VA). Take your time on each syllable. Chant the word three times. Then, still with your eyes closed, watch what happens. You may feel a kinesthetic movement, you may sense a smell, a taste, you may have an image. This is the manifestation of your "new destination." When you feel the movement is complete, breathe out and open your eyes.

Get yourself a notebook for this exercise and entitle it "Words." You are going to write down your experience. You will find this is very help-ful. As you "exteriorize" your experience, it takes on substance in the physical world, becoming a reality of its own. (If images come to you, as well as describing them, you can also draw or paint what you see).

Whatever you experience in this exercise is very important because it is the manifestation of your new destination, just as the image of Jacob's face was the manifestation of Joseph's destination.

To etch your new destination deep within your being, chant "AHAVA," (or the word you have chosen), three times in the morning and three times at night and, if possible, at the same time every day. While you are chanting, concentrate on what is your new destination. Do this for a cycle of twenty-one days, then stop for seven days or, if you are a woman, do it from the end of one period to the beginning of your next one. Then stop for the *duration* of your period. After the seven-day pause, begin anew with a new word and a new emotion (fear, envy, greed, etc.), that you want to transmute.

It is good to continue this task for at least one year. During that time you will be able to go down the list of all the emotions you inscribed on your little notebook in chapter 2. Doing this as a regular discipline is the first step of the Master Game; the second step is to transmute the negative emotion *as soon as* the negative emotion rears its ugly head during the course of a typical day.

THE MASTER GAME

Say you have chosen to work with anger. When you reverse at night, it is important to pay special attention to how you may have displayed anger during that day. And during the *day*, be on the look-out for what you know to be the first sign of your anger as it occurs.

As soon as you sense it, rather than focusing on *it*, switch your focus instead to your new destination by remembering the word you have chosen, or the specific image, smell, taste or kinesthetic movement that defines your new destination. Cleave to your new destination and feel the feeling that it invokes.

In other words, switch your gaze from anger to love. It's like turn-ing over a picture of anger to look at a picture of love on the reverse side. This should take an instant.

As soon as you've done that, cleaved to the "good," you will feel an unusual movement in your body. It is subtle because it is more your "dream body" moving than it is your physical body. You may feel your hands tingling, your toes stretching, or your neck elongating. Each one of us has a different "sign."

Once you've discovered your sign, you'll see it is always the same. It is important for you to recognize it because it tells you that the transmutation has occurred. As soon as you feel the sign you can relax; there is nothing more to be done. Anger is gone, having been replaced by love.

This state of being will allow you to respond appropriately to the situation that triggered your anger, just as David, having moved from fear to love for his God, responded gracefully, even playfully, to the threat of Goliath. This "new dream" effortlessly guides our response.

* * *

You have chanted yourself into the heartland. If you lose it again, if you react or give in to your impulses, don't despair. Don't lose time in feeling guilty. Just seize the next opportunity to shift from Nature to Surnature and to perfect your Life Plan.

When disturbances, far from disrupting you, become gems to be mined and cut to their full glory, when you feel you have mastered the intricacies of shifting and found your "sign," move on to the twelfth and final task.

There you will learn to put the finishing touches on your ability to weave yourself in and out of the two worlds of dreaming and consciousness. Becoming accomplished in this final task will merge the two worlds into one and bring the work to completion.

A QUICK REFERENCE GUIDE TO CHAPTER 11 EXERCISES

Distinguishing between Emotions and Feelings (p. 163)

Breathe out three times. Let yourself feel an emotion such as the movement of anger. Describe it to yourself. Then, with your hand, sweep it out of your body to the left. Breathe out once. Then experience to yourself a feeling, such as the movement of love. Breathe out once. Sense and then describe to yourself the difference in physical experience between an emotion and a feeling.

Identifying Your Most Frequently Experienced Emotion: Choose an Emotion to Work With (p. 165)

Go over the list of emotions you identified in chapter 2. Distinguish the emotion that comes back most frequently. This is the emotion you will be working on for the next month. (Or, for women, during the time between two menstruations.)

Recognizing an Emotion in the Moment: You Must Learn to Identify It Beforehand (p. 166)

Breathe out once. Imagine that you are experiencing intense anger. (Or whatever emotion you choose.) Describe to yourself all of the physical manifestations of your anger. Where do you feel it in your body? What color is it? What does it feel like—is it a pressure, contraction, dissolution, weakening, or a knotting? Breathe out once. Sweep the sensation out of your body to the left. Breathe out once again and open your eyes.

Labeling the "Switch": Switch from Emotion to Feeling (p. 167)

Breathe out three times. Imagine the completely opposite sensation from the sensation of anger that you just experienced. Where is it in your body? What color is it? What does it feel like? (Expansion, dilation, tingling, lightness, etc.) Give it a name, whatever is right for you: this is your "switch" or "feeling destination." Your dreaming will tell you what to name it, for instance: love, peace, harmony, balance, quiet. Breathe out once.

Chanting to Anchor Your "Feeling Destination" (p. 173)

Once you have chosen your feeling destination and named it, practice chanting to anchor this new feeling destination. Chant the sound "Aaa" or another word of your choice.

Chanting on "MiDoRe" (p. 174)

Breathe out once. Chant the word "AHAVA" (or any other word you have chosen: see appendix 2) on the "Mi" (A), "Do" (HA), "Re" (VA). Take your time with each syllable. Chant the word three times. Then, still with your eyes closed, watch what happens. You may feel a kinesthetic movement; you may sense a smell, a taste; or an image may come to you. Just note it. When you feel that the movement is complete, breathe out and open your eyes. Chant your word three times, twice a day (morning and night) for twenty-one days, then stop for seven days. Then begin anew with a new word, and a new emotion that you want to transmute.

TWELVE

Return to Oneness

"When Jacob was brought to rest in Joseph, and so the sun was united with the moon, then there commenced a production of offspring, the progenitor being Joseph. For it is that perennially flowing stream which fructifies the earth and from which generations are propagated in the world. For the sun, even when he approaches the moon, cannot cause vegetation without the help of that grade which goes under the name of Righteous." (Tzaddik, sage)

ZOHAR II 180A

Having dropped anchor in the heartland, can we remain there? Like a ship in port, we may be able to stay for a time, but eventually the boat must lift anchor and travel on. That is a ship's nature and the reason for which it was built. Just so do we incarnate, to journey through this lifetime. We cannot stay in one place, life won't allow it. Furthermore our way is strewn, like an obstacle course, with the hurdles of physical reality.

From the beginning we must face our own limitations, with all the uncertainties and longings these breed, as they also blind us to the inner abundance we were born to. When we meet obstacles, we can either collapse or, once again rising to the occasion, search for the blue eye of the clear sky at the center of our storm.

But, having found it, we can't sit on our laurels. Staying anchored in one place results in stagnation and an eventual passiveness and diminishment that causes even our heartland to turn into dust in our mouths.

The boat of our life is made to travel the open seas. Its moorage, like the umbilical cord itself, is only temporary. True, knowing we have successfully found our heart center will be a reminder of our goals and a guidance for getting back on track. Returning to that memory gives us hope, and brings us back to port faster and more effortlessly each time we try.

But there is always a counterbalance: *As we strive over and over to return to the heart center through our dreaming, the physical world strives to unman and unbalance us and cut us off from our true feelings again and again.* That is its nature, exactly as it is the scorpion's nature to sting the turtle who is attempting to carry him across the river.

Both the turtle (dreaming) and the scorpion (consciousness) will drown if we do not dream/act our way out of the "test" Nature has devised for us. If we see our life sojourn as a training ground to develop our "higher instincts," our own brand of Surnature, we won't rage against the fates. Instead, we will use every opportunity to co-create a better life wherein dreaming and consciousness are united.

If the physical world has its teaching for us, so has the inner world. "All changes . . ." says the physical world ". . . except Change," says the inner world. Attaching ourselves to the fact that the pattern of change—not the vagaries of change—is our dreaming way, we learn to become one with the movement and to rest ourselves in the rhythm of the flow.

Dreaming, with its fluidity, has taught us to move effortlessly and playfully through it all. Movement becomes not something that comes from the outside, but a living part of our very beingness. But again the physical world intervenes, and places new obstacles and new restraints in our way, reminding us that change has serious consequences, requiring soberness. *How can we be playful and sober at the same time?*

The paradox we are faced with is that we must live in both worlds to complete the great work. But how can the two worlds, so fundamentally opposite in every way, support and sustain each other? In the words of an ancient paradox, how do we get a million angels to stand on the head of a pin?

Your tasks in this book make an incremental progression towards accomplishing the ultimate goal: activating and balancing the two worlds so that hypertrophy of either one is avoided. Consciousness now comes closer to penetrating the night dream, our instinctual nature, our past through Reversing, while dreaming flowers in daylight, in an experimental and controlled environment, through Guided Exercises and Waking Dreams. Can male-directed consciousness and female-intuitive dreaming come to delight in each other's differences and grow from each other's strengths? Can they merge and separate and merge again in a perfect marriage of collaboration? What is needed to complete the work?

* * *

REVERSING AS A STATE OF MIND

At this end-point we are no longer talking of practicing, but of engaging in the real thing. You are trained and you must now enter the fray to prove yourself. Although you still have a task to perform in this final chapter, the task is precisely to help you graduate from training to mastership. This is your initiation.

To be playful while sober, imaginative while responsible, (having learned to "respond," you are now on the road to true "responsibility"), how does it work? You have had a taste of this paradox when each world, while maintaining its very own attributes, steps into the other's shoes: dreaming to perform in the conscious world, consciousness present in the dream world.

The *chassé-croisé* of reversing, no longer as an exercise but as a dance, an intimate way of being, is the first step towards embodying this paradox. At this juncture, exercises are not essential, although I will give you some.

You must teach yourself to "instinctively" and continually reverse your two modes of thinking. This has revolutionary consequences. When the pauper becomes king for a day, and the king, relinquishing his throne and his royal robes, is thrown out on the streets to fend for himself, each learns more in that one day than he ever would in a lifetime without the change. Nothing after that will ever be the same. The king emerges from the experience chastened and wiser, having experienced for himself the ills and abuses of poverty and the joys of freedom and of kindness when they have come his way. The pauper learns the weight of "responsibility," the fierce pleasures of power, the uncertainty of being loved for himself.

Having performed this unusual chassé-croisé, they both return to their known habitat (the pauper to pauperism, the king to kingship) but with something added, a remnant of the other's quality caught fast in the net of experience. The exercise has invigorated and enlivened both the pauper and the king. As their eyes meet, I imagine a creative dialogue ensues. From here on they will always retain some sense of being touched by the other's reality.

FROM CONFLICT TO PARADOX

The dual nature of our physical reality is clear to us all. We live immersed in it. There is no king without his subjects. No light without the darkness to help us distinguish it. No knowing ourselves unless we know the separation between ourselves and others. No propelling ourselves forward unless we push away from the ground. Is it any wonder that our life is a constant see-saw between opposing tendencies, with one tendency always desiring to overpower the other? This is the nature of the world we live in.

However, a world also lives in us whose laws are the complete opposite of this. In this world no opposition exists, because boundaries are insubstantial. Forms flow into each other, merge, borrow, transmute, dissolve, all in playful abandon.

In most people these two worlds have traditionally not lived happily side by side. A power struggle has existed between them from time immemorial. Each world has known the other *only* through opposition.

But for those of you who have been practicing Reversing (see chapter 5) a rapprochement has occurred, as it must have occurred between the king and the pauper. Unless, of course, their experience just bred disgust and more opposition, which is also a possibility and a risk we take whenever we reverse. Yet we must take that risk or we will end up accepting a crassly pedestrian life, a life deformed by conflict, a life in which peace and harmony can never prevail!

Isn't it finally obvious that keeping dreaming and consciousness apart will only lead to more opposition? And eventually, if sufferance of the other cannot be maintained, will not an all-out war, and the obliteration of one of these worlds, ensue? Imagine the suffering in the realm if the king ignores the plight of his paupers.

Therefore, to truly challenge your consciousness, you must take unusual steps: bring it face-to-face with what it traditionally hates, the a-causal, the irrational. To truly educate and challenge your dreaming, confront it with what it shies away from, the stark realities of the physical world.

A consciousness that cultivates sobriety (patience, attentiveness) will be rewarded with an insight into the "laws" governing the "irrational." In the cultivation of playfulness (focused playfulness and playful will), dreaming will see its dream manifest and come into reality. Critics will extol the rationalist who crossed over as a great "visionary," while the dreamer who made her dream come true will be praised as a "realist."

But still, so often we are *either* visionaries *or* realists. Can we instead think of embracing both worlds? Of encompassing all of their challenges together? *Can we endure paradox?*

Paradox means (*para*) "beyond" + (*doxa*) "opinion," from *dokein*, "to think" in Greek. Just as we embrace our children, accepting the good and the bad in them and loving them beyond opinion, can we embrace our two worlds, supporting their differences, contradictions, and opposites equally, beyond opinion? This requires more than a rapprochement. It can't be done, of course, unless our two minds are evenly matched in strength and vividness.

We know that Reversing is the first step towards perfecting that balance: consciousness agrees to step back, dreaming to step forward. Consciousness learns humbleness from dreaming and dreaming learns focus from consciousness. Dreaming abandons chaotic ebullience for focused transmutations, while consciousness recognizes differences but doesn't grab onto them.

Attaining balance is always precarious. We reach it and we lose it again as part of learning to find it again. The issue is not that we lose it, but how quickly we can regain it. Therefore, consider this task of balancing, (which is your task in this chapter), to be a work in progress. Perfection is of the moment only.

Having said that, what more, beyond reversing, do we need do? In bodywork, balance is achieved by equal pressure converging and diverging at the same time from all directions. Try to stand on your toes. You must push down and stretch up (divergence) while squeezing in your inner thigh muscles and pectorals (convergence). To develop a balance of the two minds, we need to experience the equally powerful divergence (sky and earth are opposites)—and convergence—of opposites. (Sky and earth can be held equally in the mind's eye.)

Living Opposites

Breathe out three times. See, feel, and live—being at the same time: king and pauper; breathe out once, sky and earth; breathe out once, light and darkness; breathe out once, live, being at the same time alive and dead. Or imagine two powerful oceans, one red, one blue, rushing into each other. Picture the clash of their meeting, the resulting jet rising high, the violet spume descending like a great open fan over the roiling waters: two cymbals struck together, an awakening, a brand new world. Breathe out once. Open your eyes.

When we open up to allow all manner of creatures, ways, and truths to exist side by side—the lamb with the tiger, the pauper with the king—understanding, wisdom, and compassion develop exponentially. The heart center is touched. It expands. It radiates. Each time we attain a balance of our two minds, our heart center expands a little more, in the image of the universe that ever expands while also moving forward, or should we say backing away from its inception?

What transforms a paradoxical doubleness into creation? An accident, a greater intensity, a redoubled focus? When a man and a woman come together and merge in the sexual act, a child may or may not be conceived. But passion, focus, and the right timing are great incentives to the "miraculous" act of creation. Without kavanah—the motivational force triggered by emotional ferment—creation may not occur. Having brought all the elements together we can only "let go and let God!"

In the experimental alembic that is the womb or the mind is formed the new creation, a mixing of two seemingly incompatible parts. The child looks like the father *and* like the mother, but how? The mix confuses the eye, amuses, astounds, disjoints, and unbalances our preconceived notions. Our hearts leap at the surprising freedom of the creative force to break inflexible boundaries, to mix incompatible forms. The shift, so shocking, so exciting, liberates our "True Imagination."

Imagination purified, pure love.

Love pours out an ocean to merge with that other ocean of fluid which contains unsettling forms that then become the new child; the child in turn embraces its myriad possibilities and paradoxes, untrammeled as yet with expectations and desires for its future. Love is the nectar that flows from a perfect balancing of the two minds in contemplation before the miracle of creation.

> *The wolf shall dwell with the lamb,*
> *The leopard lie down with the kid;*
> *The calf, the beast of prey, and the fatling together*
> *With a little boy to herd them.*
> *The cow and the bear shall graze,*
> *Their young shall lie down together;*
> *And the lion, like the ox, shall eat straw.*
> *A babe shall play*
> *Over a viper's hole,*
> *And an infant pass his hand*
> *Over an adder's den.*
> *In all of My sacred mount*
> *Nothing evil or vile shall be done;*
> *For the land shall be filled with devotion to the Lord*
> *As water covers the sea.*
>
> ISAIAH 11:6–9

When the two minds of dreaming and consciousness merge, their children, born of the clash of disjointed elements, may be laughter, or poetry, music, or tragedy. The ancient Greeks called these "mind children" the Muses. Hybrid forms accompany the Muses wherever they go: mermaid, centaur, flying horse, sphinx, phoenix. Riddles, enigmas, word puns, jokes, unexpected juxtapositions, leaping images jump out of the cornucopia of their being.

Transcending the ordinary, tapping the source, bringing forth the new, they jolt us out of habitual patterns into the unexpected. For, in the mind's alembic, the contraposition of these two worlds often produces shocking, paradoxical, surprising, humorous, absurd, even miraculous effects.

Coming face-to-face with the Muses is always an experience: the world as you know it stops. You are called to attention, confronted, and provoked by the new. You may want to ignore or reject what your

Muse offers, but you will still have to deal with your reactions. Faced with impossibility, irrationality, too great a joy, your body/mind may lose definition, collapse, or undergo what seems like a fainting fit, but keep conscious!

Watch as you step into the no-man's land of male-female, right-left brain oneness. Your confusion is not of the banal sort, but actually a result of co-fusion! When you are conscious/dreaming, you may feel yourself plummeting into a cushiony white light where Time stands still, noises are muffled, intimacy resides. Or amazement sears through you, like a white heat, a rousing "aha!" Co-fusion rushes you away from the horizontal, away from space-things towards the Now-eternal. It is always experienced as a vertical movement: down to rest, or up in ecstasy.

BRIDGE OVER TROUBLED WATERS

How do you prepare yourself for co-fusion? Plunged into a ferment of contradictions and possibilities, you must learn to retain your soberness. Wide-eyed and clear-browed like the god, you must learn to flow with the conflicting clues, infuriating setbacks, irrational leaps forward, ups and downs, while not sinking into panic.

It is easier said than done, of course. If you are fifty-five, female, and have no mate, if the doctor says you have a 40-percent chance of recovery, if you have lost your job and can't pay your taxes, aren't you entitled to panic? Yet here is exactly where soberness enters the picture. If you are not sober, how will you be level-headed enough to "see" and follow the "dream" clues? Like God who "hovered over the waters" (Genesis 1:2) you also must hover over your *tohu va vohu*, i.e., "chaos."

Just as in the Waking Dream your sober watching of the effervescence contributes to stabilizing the forms, so it is with your life. Instead of letting yourself be drowned in fear or paralyzed by indecision as your mind tries to sort out clues from an overabundance of stimuli, school yourself to *watch*.

This is difficult, for in moments of crisis the world outside of you seems to lose its well-established stability and appears to mimic the excessive flux and malleability, absurdity, and ebullience of your dream world. But remember: you have been trained to *respond* to dream fluidity. When your life takes on a "nightmarish" quality or a "magical" hue you are very close to co-fusion. Will you panic or keep your cool? And if you *accomplish* co-fusion, can you maintain it? Few of us ever die at the joy of seeing our new creation or our new child. Enduring the shock of the mix, we are able to stabilize our response. But can we still keep our sense of wonder intact?

How easily do we exchange one modality for the other? For instance, having internalized a new infant's looks into our consciousness, we soon lose the wonder of its newness and changeability. Or being too emotionally impressionable, we lose ourselves in contemplation of the freshness and malleability of the infant's spirit, while forgetting sometimes to respond to its physical needs.

But luckily for us, both worlds are insistent upon capturing our attention. Just as the infant cries to get our attention, (on a faster rhythm than our breathing, which is an irritant impossible to ignore), so the Muses call attention to themselves by repetition, insistent calls, and shocking behavior. When we are ready for a new configuration, a new "reality," the mind—unknowing of its own mechanisms—begins to search for and latch onto patterns, similarities, symbolism, simultaneity, and synchronicities everywhere.

But here let us pause for a moment of needed sobriety: are these synchronicities the doing of our minds only? Or are there actually synchronicities out there? Is the outer world involved and participating in creating these clues just for us; toying with us, teasing us, waving its sudden clusters of meaning before our noses like red flags? *Does the universe move to our stories as we move to its events?* Could the outer world have a purpose that responds to ours and moves us along too, just as air, moved by depressions and cold fronts, is also moved by the sucking action of our lungs? Is the world more malleable than we are willing to admit?

If dream is a potential physical reality—and we have seen that it is (chapter 8)—in retrospect can physical reality also be a potential dream? If so, its fixity is less fixed than we had thought. All clearly depends on the relationship: how our minds are inclined determines the nature of the clues we focus on in the outer world.

These, in turn, seem to spring to attention as if on cue. In turn, they affect our inner condition. The more actively we go back and forth between the two worlds, the more apt we are to co-fuse, and thus discover a new level of reality. *Can we dare imagine that physical determinism may be shifted by dreaming?* Can we risk the hope that "Faith (actually) moves mountains"?

One of the difficulties of our physical incarnation is habits. How tiresome they are and yet how difficult it is to escape their grasp! But if we bring our sober attention to the patterns and new configurations, the signs and clues that the mind and world conjoined present us with, we may escape our base conditioning and, like the gods, (although not *ex nihilo*) create newness.

Watch for the clues. Follow them and they will lead you through the crack in-between the worlds. Turn the little gold key in the lock, push open the secret door, slide through the sliver of light. You have already forayed into this world. It is, of course, the heartland where True Imagination—love—reigns supreme.

Enter that state of being and experience how effortlessly your dreaming flows into physical reality and affects it with its special brand of playful ease and magic, while your consciousness, unperturbed, pursues its focus through the paradisiacal haze, bringing solidity and tangible manifestations to the dreaming.

But, please, don't rest upon your laurels, don't think you will live happily ever after! That only happens in fairy tales. The vanity of such thought or some other perturbation will tip us out of the heartland, presenting us with yet another opportunity to re-conquer it and to expand it. Total illumination is not of this world: there are always new causes for unbalance, and new heart spaces to grow into.

REVERSING TRICKS

Give yourself a treat: hop on a plane to England, as my son and I did last year. As you deplane, it is dawn in Heathrow, whereas for you it still feels like the dead of night and you have hardly slept.

Rent a car: they only have non-automatics there. Suddenly you are driving on the left side of the road, seated on the right, changing gears with your left hand, trying to habituate your eyes to look left for the road signs and right for ongoing cars. Then drive into a huge April snowstorm, as we did, and you'll laugh yourselves silly trying to keep up with all the manual reversing and mind twisting. But you have to be sober too, no accidents please!

I hope they never change the road systems in England. As if birthed from that initial shock of laughter, our trip unfolded like a dream: we just happened on humorous, unusual, or angelic people, on the best restaurants, the quaintest hotels, amazing, hidden sites, paradisiacal gardens. Yet we did not deviate too far from our proposed itinerary, which kept us grounded in objective reality.

Imagine our itinerary as a straight line, our dreaming as a meandering curve crossing and re-crossing that straight line. On our trip we accomplished all we had set out to do, but our spontaneous acceptance of new clues and other possibilities gave color and joy to our experience.

Physical Reversing

Any reversing of the usual will do for exercise: visiting a country where you don't speak the language, eating a food you have never tasted before, participating in a sport you think you'll hate. Try them because they are the opposite of what you would normally do. Of course, don't deliberately reverse just for the sake of reversing, for turning it into a willful process will land you in a tangle.

Always stay within the dreaming flow and follow the dream clues within, and those amazing synchronicities, simultaneities, and opportunities in the outer world will never cease to amaze you. For instance, three people in one day talk to you about a sailing trip. You're struck by the coincidence. The next day you bump into an old friend you haven't seen in ages. He talks to you about a sailing trip! In fact, he's in town to board a ship sailing down to the Caribbean, but its departure has been postponed because one of the crew members desisted at the last moment.

Here's your dreaming clue, your opportunity! You're free for the next few weeks, at loose ends yourself, and you have always wanted to take a sailing trip! Don't go searching for it but, if an opportunity presents itself, go for it! Switch your energy from indecision and idle irritation (when presented with the "cue") to active participation in the flow.

Take the risk! If you don't, you'll always wonder what you missed.

This is not about forcing yourself to do the opposite of what you like to do but of catching the tail end of the dreaming.

Meanwhile, as an exercise, start with manual reversing. I have an old house deep in the woods on a small, one-lane dirt road. When another car comes along, one of us must back up. Experience on that dirt road has shown me that most people don't know how. Learn to back up flawlessly and fast! There should be no difference between your forward or backward driving. Practice that.

Or learn to use your left hand, (or right hand if you are a lefty), in your tennis game, fencing, golf, or drawing. A poet friend of mine always switched hands when her writing got stale. Some parts of a poem, or sometimes a complete poem, were written by her left-handed self. Her writer's block was knocked off-balance, swept away by the new wind of her right brain inspiration. (The left hand is governed by the right brain.)

It's a great thing when you realize you still have the ability to surprise yourself or be surprised by the outside world.

* * *

AWAKE IN SLEEP

Remember Nut, the Egyptian goddess of the night? Each dusk she swallows the sun. All night, the sun travels through the great sky arc of her body to be born anew between her legs each dawn. If we look at ancient illustrations of the goddess, the sun in her dark embrace is as resplendent as it is in the sky. Yet while its light shines, it doesn't obliterate the darkness. This is Nut's mystery and her great power: she can accommodate the light in the darkness while remaining true to her godhood.

For is she not protectoress of the fecund darkness? What is this paradox that she offers for our contemplation? Can we learn more from her about bringing consciousness into the dream time? Can consciousness travel through the night of the dream time, "see," and yet not destroy? Can consciousness be active without willing us to awaken?

So far, reversing has taught you to bring your consciousness close to the moment of sleep but not to actually have it travel through your sleep (chapter 5). As the young hero, Conscious Mind Courageous, you must now advance even closer to the gaping black hole of oblivion.

Be Awake When Falling Asleep

Your kavanah is to be watchful as you fall asleep. Pay attention to the exact moment of your sinking into sleep. At first you will be felled by sleep before you even realize it is happening. Then one night, if you persevere, lo and behold! You are falling asleep before your very eyes; you can actually describe to yourself the physical changes that happen at that moment. For me, falling asleep means my jaws click together: that is my sign. For you it may be something different. Just watch until you are there, conscious, in the moment of transition. Try it also in the morning, as you awaken. Tell yourself, the night before, to be conscious of the moment of transition between sleep and waking. Watch the physical signs, but also watch your thinking process begin to invade the wisps of your still-unfolding dream images. Try to retain both, don't let your waking drown and obliterate the dream.

Being awake during transitions is a form of sobriety that prepares you for the final transition. Wouldn't you want to be aware through the dying process? To plummet the great mystery? But wait, we still have exciting things to do in this lifetime, such as teaching ourselves to actually be conscious within our dream time. Can we, like the sun, travel through Nut's body, aware and awake *in* our sleep?

Be Awake in the Dream Time

Do this before starting your Reversing exercise, lying in bed, eyes closed. Tell yourself to be aware that you are dreaming as you dream by instructing yourself to say (in your dream): "I am dreaming this."

Persevere in telling yourself this every night and checking every morning whether, yes, you did in fact realize within your dream time that, "I am dreaming this." It is not difficult to accomplish. When you get good at this exercise you can make it happen every night. You will also become aware that you are feeling very much awake in your dream time.

When this is the case, you can easily move on to the next exercise: learning to face the necessities, responding to the challenges of the dream *during* dream time, instead of waiting for the morning to do so as you have done so far.

Responding to the Dream Challenge during Dream Time

Many times during the day you have practiced responding to the dream challenge. Try now to respond directly to your dream's necessity in the dream time. Say in the dream: "This is my dream," knowing these are your images and you are responsible for how you choose to meet them. Then expand upon the previous exercise by responding actively and appropriately to the dream challenge and its necessity as soon as it presents itself to you in the dream.

When I first met Colette, I was very sick, being so far gone into the mists of dreaming I no longer felt the world around me. As you can tell from that description, I wasn't the least bit sober! Because I had lost my grounding in outer reality, the playfulness of dreaming eluded me too. In fact, I thought I was dying. Every night I had terrible nightmares.

Colette's remedy: clean! If it's dirty on the inside, then clean on the outside. Clean the terrace, the floors, polish the copper pots and trays, (of which were a great many in Colette's North African sixteenth-century decor!), and the silverware. Weed the garden, trim the bushes, empty the trash. I was lucid enough to know she wasn't using me but teaching me something. And I soon learned what.

One night I had, as usual for that time, a nightmare. But instead of waking in a sweat and a panic, I heard myself saying: "This is my dream!" and taking up my imaginal bucket and brush (as I had so many times in reality), I cleaned the darkness out of the dream!

When you have become proficient in meeting the dream directly you can dialogue with it. The technique is similar.

Dialoguing with Your Dream

Before Reversing, lie in bed, eyes closed. Breathe out three times, counting from three to one. Imagine that, with a gold pen, you draw a circle of gold light in the darkness. Within the circle, write your question to your dream, in letters of gold light. For instance: "Am I pregnant?" If that is indeed your most pressing question of the moment the dream will certainly give you an answer. If it is not really the most pressing, you will receive an answer to what, in fact, is. You cannot fool the dream world. Make sure in the morning that you record every detail of your dream with precision. We have a way of manipulating our images to suit our wishes, especially if we haven't written them down.

To be awake in one's sleep is a unique sensation. At first you may feel you haven't had a good night's sleep. Soon the contrary sensation will settle in. You will feel very rested and very clear. Your life cycle from sleep, to waking, to sleep, will feel seemly and smooth. Eventually, consciousness will pervade even the non-imaging moments of your sleep.

DREAMING AWAKE

At first, dreaming while you're awake doesn't seem so difficult. You are able to conjure up worlds in your mind, whether these are memories, daydreams, or fantasies, and you have also learned to visualize. All these happenings are dream-related because they are linked to the activation of the Imagination. But daydreams and fantasies are led by *willful* thinking, and are not to be confused with spontaneous dreaming. As for the visualizations you have practiced, they are only exercises to help stimulate your True Imagination. It is time now to see your Imagination in spontaneous activity.

Since we have hypothesized that we also dream during the daytime, (and we have proved that we can provoke dreaming through exercises and Waking Dreams) can we catch glimpses or whole sequences of the spontaneous dreaming that goes on behind the scenes, while simultaneously remaining fully conscious? Sometimes, under heavy stress, the imaginal world bursts forth and breaks like a bubble at the surface of our daytime consciousness.

But generally in a healthy person, daytime dreaming is as indistinct as the pale moon in a sunlit sky. Sometimes we catch glimpses of a full-scale image, or an audited message, while sometimes we just intuit them. But, for the most part, we don't pay attention to these tenuous offerings from the dream world. How can we improve on our daytime dream sighting during the time when consciousness blazes forth triumphant, bathing everything on its passage in light?

The Zohar (the thirteenth-century, most celebrated kabbalistic text) tells us that when God created the sun and the moon, the moon, seeing the sun's magnificence, grew jealous when comparing its fire to her soft white glow. She complained to God, who punished her ill-humor by diminishing her size and her light, making her dependent on the reflective light of the sun. But as we are told, the day the moon grows as big and resplendent as the sun is the day the world will be perfected.

The moon, of course, is your dreaming. It waxes and wanes in your awareness and at times disappears altogether, exactly like the moon. The sun is your consciousness, fiercely protective of its prerogatives and not about to let your dreaming encroach on its well-guarded preserves.

Since it is no use trying to compete with consciousness, why not elicit its cooperation? Why not use it to watch, not only the outer world which it does by predilection, but also the inner world? One eye looks out, one eye looks in or, if you prefer, you can imagine your eyes as spherical mirrors that are equally able to see in and out.

Dream images, as you know, are elusive. Any pressure on your part and they dissolve. Like wisps of smoke, they take shape then drift apart too quickly to be insighted, unless you are delicate in your watching! Unless, like a hunter you tread softly, making no noise, (no mind noises), while pursuing your quarry with relentless but silent intensity. The forest is full of game and if you can blend in with the trees and the landscape you will soon see the shy, secretive animal world at play.

Insight Outsight

Imagine that you have one eye looking out, one eye looking in. Or, if you prefer, imagine your eyes as spherical mirrors that see out and in at the same time. Either way, become aware of the double movement of your looking. While never losing sight of what is happening in the outer world, (this is extremely important as the tendency when dreaming is to lose oneself in the dreaming) watch also what is happening in your inner world. Watch the images, the sayings that rise spontaneously on your inner screen/tape. Don't try to interpret them, simply let your consciousness absorb them. If you allow them to sit untroubled in your mind, soon their meaning will come to you.

There is a very particular look to the eyes of those who master this double movement. Once you identify that look you will never forget it: the eyes are paradoxically both piercing and deep, with a dry core, yet liquid. It is the look you find in sages' eyes but also in clairvoyants' eyes. Why so? Because clairvoyance is the first consequence of practicing this double vision. And yes, it will happen to you too! But don't pay too much attention to your ESP, except as a mark of your progress on the road to becoming a true dreamer.

When your mirror is clear, even if only for a moment, (no claims, expectations, desires, wants), your imagination responds truthfully to what you see in the outer world. It is as simple as that. Remember that True Imagination, acting somewhat like a reverse mirror image, has a way of showing up the quirky, of illuminating the hidden aspects you don't habitually focus on.

Being interactive, it has an infinitely more complex way of manifesting than a flat mirrored surface does and, like the paintings in Harry Potter's magical world, it will wave back at you! This is similar to your night dreams which will often highlight the aspects of your daily life that you had not consciously paid attention to during your waking hours.

Imagine you are standing in the center of a spherical room which is entirely covered with mirrors: neither side could directly reflect *all* of you. Each side would have to depend upon the other side for a complete picture. Exactly so does dreaming, the twin pendant to your consciousness, show up what your consciousness has missed.

SPEAKING FROM THE DREAMWORLD

As with all things pertaining to the inner world, having identified your dreaming during waking hours, you must bring it forward into the physical world to ground its impact. Faithful to the Reversing (the back and forth of dreaming into consciousness, consciousness into dreaming) that is the keystone to this work, you must act or speak your insight.

Or, if you choose to keep quiet in the immediate, that too must be a conscious act, one that does not obliterate the message but stores it up for future reference. But remember that you will be consigning your dreaming to fantasy if you cannot brave Aristotelian scorn, just as your conscious thinking would be reduced to sterile logic if it refused to embrace the a-causality and the mystery of the dream world. As our most renowned scientist, Albert Einstein, was wont to say, "Imagination is more important than knowledge."

To bring your daytime dreaming into the world, you must learn to speak your dream insights out loud. Don't try to translate your images into a logical sequence, don't shy away from a non-sequitur. Just stay with what it is you "see." Stay with the language of "seeing" and describe it as you would describe a physical landscape. Stay close to your source.

For instance, suppose you meet a beautiful woman and, as you assess her with your critical left brain, you are also "dreaming" your response to her. Let's say your dreaming response is to "see" a field of poppies. What does the field mean? And why poppies? Don't let these logical questions cloud or complicate your insight. Let the image sit with you, caress you, inform you. And then speak up and say to the beautiful woman: "When I see you I am reminded of a field of poppies." She may blush but she'll be touched because, as you know, the language of images—the wordless language—is also the language of emotions and feeling.

If it is not appropriate to speak thus to her, (for she has a jealous husband who might think you're coming on to her) store the dream image for future reference. Don't consign it to oblivion. The knowledge gained from the image "field of poppies" (heady beauty, intoxication, passion, grace) might come in useful later on.

What if you see a *negative* image? At this point in your practice you know you are no longer projecting secondary emotions, so you can trust your inner eye. Suppose you "see" dark blotchy red all around your friend, simply say: "When I see you I am seeing red all around you. Are you angry or upset about something?"

In other words, speak directly *from* the dream image instead of short-circuiting half of your brain's input. When you learn to use both your left brain and your right brain to feed your conversation, it makes for much more enlivening exchanges.

Speaking from the Dreaming

Using the double-eye movement, see within as well as without when you are conversing with another person. Then practice speaking from both sources, the left brain critical and the right brain dreaming. Use both inputs. Since it is the dreaming input which is generally lacking, concentrate on expressing that side of your thinking whenever you engage another person in conversation.

At first you may find this embarrassing or difficult to do, but persevere. You will see people perk up, light up, become friendly. The inner intuitive language, when communicated, opens up doors to people's hearts and minds, as it has opened up doors in you. Your daring and fluidity will be appreciated.

Practice speaking from your "insights" and soon your two languages will blend. You will have created for yourself a new, fresh, and very alive way of communicating. It will free you from calculation and manipulation. The grace, ease, and magic of dreaming will animate all of your encounters.

* * *

THE SECRET OF LIFE

Once upon a time there was a man who traveled all over the earth in search of the answer to one question: "What is the secret of life?" He put this question to philosophers, mathematicians, astronomers, astrologers, seers, sages, saints, gurus, all to no avail. The answers he got did not satisfy his longing. He was tired, disillusioned, and bitter when he finally reached a small village at the foot of a mountain. There the villagers pointed to a tall mountaintop.

So the traveler set off one last time to climb the mountain. At the summit sat a little old man, shriveled and smiling. "The secret of life is a fountain!" said he.

The traveler was incensed. "I haven't come this far to be told it's a fountain!"

"Well, isn't it?" queried the little old man.

If, like the traveler, you have come this far in your reading but haven't done the practices, you too may feel as if you are still searching, not happy with my answers, disillusioned and bitter. I could insist till doomsday that when you balance consciousness and dreaming, when your two languages blend and become one, you will feel the life force bubbling up within you. You will experience joy, fun, and exhilaration. The fountain will rise in you! But why should I try to convince you? You must find this out for yourself.

If you haven't yet felt life's joy rising like a clear fountain in you, you may need to repeat some of the tasks described in this book. Remember that Imagination is a timeless world, and it is always there. Although, in order to simplify my task and yours, I have sequenced the work and organized it into twelve parts; you must undertake all of its tasks simultaneously. This is not as difficult as it may seem, for when you are familiar with all the tasks, you will naturally want to incorporate them into one fluid practice.

What are the signs strewn along your way that tell you that you are progressing in the right direction? Those I could not begin to tell you before, for fear of influencing your "seeing." But if you have come this far and faithfully done the practices, you will surely recognize the signs I am about to describe.

Remember the story of the sun and the moon? When you first start your practices, your dreams are a reflection of your everyday life, just as the light of the moon is a reflection of the sun's light. Your dreams are busy dreams, nightmares, or recurring dreams. Their light waxes and wanes, dims and darkens because you haven't yet stabilized your emotions or learned to shift to feelings.

As you practice clearing the past and cleaning daily events, as you stimulate your Imagination through exercises, a magical thing happens: the moon inside you starts to glow with its own light. Imaginings which were once dark, dense, heavy, enclosed, chaotic, apathetic, or else too ethereal, evanescent, elusive, or unstable, now become clear, sharp, and clean. Mixed colors disappear and are replaced by pure colors. Movement is fluid and quicksilver. New configurations occur easily. Transformations surprise, amaze, and delight.

As you continue to practice, pure colors move from the darker ranges to the lighter, clearer, more pastel. They become transparent and then luminous. Even when visualizing darkness, the black is not dense, but translucent and luminous. A radiance shines through all forms; they glitter and glow with light.

Eventually the forms fuse into the light, losing their boundaries, and all becomes one glowing whiteness. The heart, mind, and body expand into this boundaryless radiance, into transparency. The practitioner is illumined and becomes one with the universe.

Is this the end work? The joining of sun and moon, of consciousness and dreaming? No. To finalize the work, the practitioner must come down off the mountain, the light to be brought down into physical reality, grounded in proper conduct and humility. The dance of interweaving must not cease. Do not rest but continue reinventing yourself until your last breath, and life will not cease to surprise you with its fluidity, ease, and abundance.

If, as time goes on, you come to a place where you think you have lost the paradisiacal light, always remember that you once found it by actively balancing your two worlds, and that it can always be found again. It never ceases to be an ideal worth striving for. Don't ever give up your right to return!

When the sun and the moon fuse and become one, the work is perfected. The light lives within you and through you day and night. Even in your deepest, dreamless sleep you *know* the light. Consciousness and dreaming are alive in you at all times.

You were once buffeted by outer and inner forces but now you have learned to become the master of their movements. Whenever, if only for an instant, you can touch the still center of movement, you will be complete. Sit quietly in its center, while simultaneously not ceasing to flow with the movement: paradise has come to earth! The garden of your heart is open and aglow!

A QUICK REFERENCE GUIDE TO CHAPTER 12 EXERCISES

Living Opposites: Teaching Yourself to Live Comfortably with Paradox (p. 184)

Breathe out three times. See, feel, and live being king and pauper at the same time. Breathe out once. See, feel, and live being sky and earth at the same time. Breathe out once. See, feel, and live being light and darkness at the same time. Breathe out once. See, feel, and live being at the same time alive and dead. Breathe out once. Open your eyes.

Physical Reversing: Learn to Reverse in Every Physical Way That You Can Think Of (p. 189)

Practice manual reversing by switching hands when playing tennis or golf, or when fencing, drawing, writing—or learn to back up perfectly when driving, etc. Follow the dream clues both within yourself and in the world outside. Watch for the synchronicities, simultaneities, and opportunities that the dream flow presents and don't hesitate to seize them.

Be Awake When Falling Asleep (p. 191)

Be watchful as you fall asleep. Pay attention to the exact moment that you sink into sleep. Breathe out once. Try this also as you awaken. The night before, tell yourself to be conscious of the moment of transition between sleep and waking. Don't let the waking drown and obliterate the memory of your dream.

Be Awake in the Dream Time (p. 191)

Do this before starting your Reversing exercise, when you are lying in bed with your eyes closed. Tell yourself to be aware that you are dreaming as you dream, and to say in your dream: "I am dreaming this."

Responding to the Dream Challenge during Dream Time (p. 192)

Many times during the daytime practices you have responded to the dream challenge. Do so now directly in the dream time. Say in the dream: "This is my dream," knowing these are your images and you are responsible for how you choose to meet them. Then respond appropriately to the dream challenge.

Dialoguing with Your Dream: Learn to Ask Your Dreams Important Questions (p. 193)

Before Reversing, lay in bed, with your eyes closed, and breathe out three times. Imagine yourself, with a gold pen, drawing a circle of light in the darkness. Within the circle, direct your question to your dream in letters of gold light. For instance: "Am I pregnant?" If that is indeed your most pressing question of the moment, the dream will certainly give you an answer to it. If it is not really the most pressing question, you will receive an answer to what, in fact, is. You cannot fool the dream world. Make sure that, in the morning, you record every detail of your dream with precision.

Insight Outsight: Learn to Look at the Dream Images while Focusing on the Outer World (p. 195)

While never losing sight of what is happening in the outer world, watch also what is happening in your inner world. Watch the images, and the sayings that arise spontaneously on your inner screen/tape. Don't try to interpret them, simply let your consciousness absorb them.

Speaking from the Dreaming: Practice Speaking Aloud Your Dream Images (p. 197)

Using the double-eye movement, see within, as well as without, when you are conversing with another person. Then practice speaking from both sources, the left brain critical and the right brain dreaming. Use both inputs. Since it is the dreaming input which is generally lacking, concentrate on expressing that side of your thinking as well whenever you engage another person in conversation.

APPENDIX 1

Example of a Set of Exercises

Here is an example of a class in Guided Exercises. When you do these exercises, do them all at one sitting. Then write down what you saw.

THE RAINBOW BRIDGE

1. See, feel, and live that after the storm comes the purifying rain, after the deluge the rainbow.
2. See a drop of water hanging from a cloud. Enter the drop, go to the center. What do you find?
3. See, feel, live how the rainbow is the bridge between God and you.
4. See, know why the rainbow is God's manifest sign that Man will be spared another Great Flood.
5. Imagine climbing up a staircase, each step is one of the colors of the rainbow. As you step onto the red step hear the sound of red, feel it in all your body, see the image the red evokes for you, breathe out once; step onto orange, breathe out once; step onto yellow, breathe out once; step onto green, breathe out once; step onto blue, breathe out once; step onto indigo, breathe out once; step onto purple.
6. Now come down the staircase. Sense, see, feel being clothed in all seven colors of the staircase. Hear the symphony they make.
7. Sense, see, feel that the many colored tunic is the Mother's (the

Shechina's) embrace. Breathe out once. See, know why without it our physical body withers like a plant deprived of water.

8. Sense a place of pain in your body. Look at the color of your pain. Breathe out twice. Place your hands above the pain. Watch what happens to the color.

9. Visualize people you are close to. Recognize and admit to yourself negative emotions you have about some of them. Recognize for yourself where there is irritation, anger, envy, jealousy, fear. See your emotion and name it to yourself exactly as it is. Do not try to pretend otherwise. Breathe out once. See the color of your emotion, how it projects out, how it creates a protective shield between you and that person. Breathe out twice. Take three steps back, watch your emotions change. What do you see, what happens?

10. See, know that the darkening of colors comes from separation. Breathe out twice. See, live what is concealed behind your envy of another.

11. See, feel, know what you are really competing about. Breathe out twice. Have you ever felt hate? Recognize it and its color.

12. See, feel, know why the Mother (the Shechina) is often concealed in black garments. Breathe out once. See live and know why it is said that because of Joseph the Red Sea parted for the Hebrews. What does this tell you about transforming emotions?

13. Sense, see, feel how emotions change your breathing. Experience your breathing when in fear, anger, envy, hate. Breathe out twice. How do you breathe when having feelings of awe, love, gratitude, victory? Breathe out once. Live and know how returning to a natural rhythm of breathing you are restoring the Covenant between you and God.

14. Visualize passing your hands over your body from your feet up all the front of your body. Imagine that you are caressing the colors of your aura. Watch how you breathe and feel, and how your colors change. What happens to your body? Breathe out once. See yourself clothed in iridescence.

Words for Chanting (Shemot)

Here is a comprehensive list of WORDS you can choose from for your chanting. Use the Hebrew transliteration. Chant on MI DO RE. If you don't find the word that best describes your new destination, choose an English word that fits. Or, if you have a knowledge of Hebrew, it is always best to use the Hebrew word. When you have a word with only two syllables, chant the first syllable twice, once on MI and once on DO. CH is a hard guttural sound.

Abundance	SHEFA	שֶׁפַע
Awakening	H'ARAH	הֶאָרָה
Beginning	BERESHIT	בְּרֵאשִׁית
Bliss	ONEG	עֹנֶג
Calmness	SHALVAH	שַׁלְוָה
Charity	TZEDAKAH	צְדָקָה
Clarity	BEHIRUT	בְּהִירוּת
Compassion	CHEMLAH	חֶמְלָה
Conceptualization	B'RI'YAH	בְּרִיאָה
Confidence	BITACHON	בִּטָּחוֹן

Courage	OMETZ	אֹמֶץ
Creation	YETZIRAH	יְצִירָה
Differentiation	HAVDALAH	הַבְדָּלָה
Faith	EMUNAH	אֱמוּנָה
Forward	KADIMAH	קָדִימָה
Happiness	SIMCHAH	שִׂמְחָה
Innocence	TEMIMUT	תְּמִימוּת
Joy	SASSON	שָׂשׂוֹן
Life	CHAYIM	חַיִּים
Love	AHAVAH	אַהֲבָה
Loving kindness	CHESED	חֶסֶד
Mercy	RACHAMIM	רַחֲמִים
Order	SEDER	סֵדֶר
Patience	SAVLANUT	סַבְלָנוּת
Peace	SHALOM	שָׁלוֹם
Precision	DE'YUK	דִּיּוּק
Realization	ASI'YAH	עֲשִׂיָּה
Remember	Z'CHOR	זְכוֹר
Return/Repentance	TESHUVAH	תְּשׁוּבָה
Sign	SIMAN	סִימָן
Straight	YASHAR	יָשָׁר
Silence	SHEKET	שֶׁקֶט
Success	HATZLACHAH	הַצְלָחָה
Tranquility	MENUCHAH	מְנוּחָה
Wholeness	SHALEM	שָׁלֵם

BOOKS OF RELATED INTEREST

The World Dream Book
Use the Wisdom of World Cultures to Uncover Your Dream Power
by Sarvananda Bluestone, Ph.D.

Dreamways of the Iroquois
Honoring the Secret Wishes of the Soul
by Robert Moss

The World Is As You Dream It
Shamanic Teachings from the Amazon and Andes
by John Perkins

The Prophet's Way
A Guide to Living in the Now
by Thom Hartmann

The Shamanic Way of the Bee
Ancient Wisdom and Healing Practices of the Bee Masters
by Simon Buxton

Kabbalistic Healing
A Path to an Awakened Soul
by Jason Shulman

The Secret Doctrine of the Kabbalah
Recovering the Key to Hebraic Sacred Science
by Leonora Leet, Ph.D.

The Kabbalah of the Soul
The Transformative Psychology and Practices of Jewish Mysticism
by Leonora Leet, Ph.D.

INNER TRADITIONS • BEAR & COMPANY
P.O. Box 388
Rochester, VT 05767
1-800-246-8648
www.InnerTraditions.com

Or contact your local bookseller